Parenting

About the Author

John Lonergan is a native of Bansha, Co. Tipperary. He served in the Irish Prison Service for over 42 years. He was Governor of Mountjoy Prison for over 22 years and Governor of the top security prison at Portlaoise for almost four years. He retired in June 2010 and later that year his autobiography, *The Governor*, was published.

His philosophy is that change, personal or otherwise, cannot be enforced on people, and he believes that real and meaningful change only comes about through dialogue, consent and agreement. He is convinced that people change from the inside out and suggests that the big task for all of us as human beings is to find the humanity in others and then to nurture it. He is convinced that the more people are in touch with their own humanity the more likely they are to treat others with humanity.

He is the father of two adult daughters and has two grandsons. For over twenty years he has delivered a talk to parents of school-going children called 'Parenting – The Challenges and the Rewards', sharing his personal experience of parenting.

Parenting

Raising Your Child in Ireland Today

John Lonergan

ORPEN PRESS

Published by
Orpen Press
Lonsdale House
Avoca Avenue
Blackrock
Co. Dublin
Ireland

e-mail: info@orpenpress.com
www.orpenpress.com

Paperback ISBN 978-1-909895-02-7
ePub ISBN 978-1-909895-33-1
Kindle ISBN 978-1-909895-34-8

Printed in Glasgow by Bell & Bain Ltd

To my daughters, Sinéad and Marie

Foreword

Shortly after I became a proud granddad, I was given some great advice. If you're willing to do a 4 a.m. feed, I was told, or change the smelliest nappy in the Western world, that's being a good granddad. Everything else is interference.

So writing about parenting, from that perspective, is just about as tricky a subject as you can handle. As John Lonergan says early on in this book, "Nothing causes as much stress as grandparents or other immediate relatives or close personal friends offering unsolicited advice."

So the real trick is to draw on the lessons you have learned from your own life, to apply what you know of the science of parenting but with a light touch, and to make it clear that you are an ally of the parent involved, and never a judge.

Nobody does this better than John Lonergan. I've heard him speak in public many times, and I'm always bowled over by his clarity, his passion and his simplicity. He's a natural storyteller when he's on his feet, and always leaves audiences wanting more. All of those skills are visible here.

I'm also lucky enough to have asked John Lonergan, immediately after he retired from his job as Governor of Mountjoy, to serve on the board of Barnardos. Board meetings of any organisation, even charities with a strong sense of values, can get bogged down in all the issues of governance, finances and management. But with John on our board, we never forget the reason we were all here. If we needed a social conscience, John would be it.

Mind you, he's easily enough underestimated. He presents this air sometimes of "Ah, sure what would I know? I'm only a harmless old public servant." Believe that and you'll believe anything. There's a depth of wisdom and experience under John's pleasant and unassuming exterior, and it's based on years of learning in one of the hardest schools of all.

I happen to know that John has learned, through his years as a prison governor, that if we were all the best parents we could be, the institution he ran for so many years would never have been overcrowded. For sure, the link between education, on the one hand, and poverty and disadvantage, on the other, is profound. Nothing breaks the vicious circle of poverty better than education does – and nothing hampers the educational development of a child more than poverty and disadvantage does.

In the middle of that, parenting is absolutely crucial. A parent who believes in bedtime stories is much less likely to be the parent of a child or young person who struggles with literacy. A parent who loved school when they were a kid themselves is much less likely to be the parent of a child who drops out from school early.

All these interactions, and many many more, are challenging. We all know, I think, that the stresses and strains that can crowd into our lives – whether they are caused by busy and glamorous careers, or whether they come hand-in-hand with the despair that poverty can bring in its wake – can all contribute to stopping us from being the parents we need to be. That doesn't mean we love our kids less. But it can mean that we lose the way to translate that love into effective parenting.

And of course, in the world we live in, the need for effective parenting – and the obstacles in its way – are growing exponentially. Our children are exposed to a thousand different sources of glamour, excitement, information and danger that never occurred to us when we were young. The generation that has difficulty dealing with anything more than the most basic computer tasks is bound to end up speaking a different language to the next generation.

I read recently that the term 'generation gap' was coined only around 50 years ago. It referred, among other things, to the appalled and confused reaction of that generation's parents to the phenomenon known as Elvis Presley. Originally, there had to be a gap of around twenty years between one generation and the next before the depths of that kind of misunderstanding were plumbed. Nowadays, it seems, there's a new generation gap every two years.

With all these challenges, we need to read something wise, simple, reassuring and compassionate. That is the basis on which I believe you should read this book. There is no interference here, no unsolicited advice – just a wise and decent man, offering a supportive hand on a challenging and rewarding journey.

John is very generously donating his author's royalties to both Barnardos in the Republic of Ireland and Barnardo's Northern Ireland to the benefit of all our children on this island. Lynda Wilson, Director of Barnardo's NI, and I, as the Chief Executive of Barnardos in the Republic of Ireland, wish to express our gratitude for this extremely generous gesture – and to all of you who have bought the book, you are also helping, each in your own way, to change a child's life for the better.

Fergus Finlay

CEO
Barnardos Ireland

Lynda Wilson

Director
Barnardo's Northern Ireland

Acknowledgements

Thanks to all the primary and secondary school parent associations all over Ireland who, over many years, invited me to share my parenting experience and philosophy with them. This in turn has provided me with much of the material for this book.

Thanks to all the secondary schools and colleges throughout the country for giving me the great opportunity of talking with thousands of students and exchanging views and experiences with them, again over many years. Special thanks to all the students for contributing to so many discussions and debates during my school visits. Their contributions have helped me to develop a better insight into how young people in Ireland cope with the many challenges they face day in, day out and, most importantly, how we as parents can help and support them.

Thanks to my daughters, Sinéad and Marie, for making me reflect time and time again on the views and opinions I held on many issues. They helped me in no small way to realise that parenting is a two-way learning process.

Thanks to Fergus Finlay, Chief Executive of Barnardos Ireland, and Lynda Wilson, Director of Barnardo's Northern Ireland, for writing the foreword and for allowing me to donate the royalties from the book to Barnardos.

A very special thanks to Eileen O'Brien, editor of Orpen Press, for all her expertise, patience and support during this whole process. Also, thanks to Elizabeth Brennan, who worked as editor during the early stages of the book, for all her support and encouragement.

Contents

Contents

Contents

Barnardos
www.barnardos.ie

Barnardos in Ireland

Barnardos' goal is to make Ireland the best place in the world to be a child. Every day in 40 projects across Ireland Barnardos works with almost 6,300 children and families whose lives are marred by issues such as poverty, neglect and educational disadvantage.

We support children whose well-being is under threat, by working with them, their families and communities, and by campaigning for the rights of children. For over fifty years Barnardos has worked closely with more than 100,000 children and families living in disadvantaged communities throughout Ireland, supporting them to achieve their potential in life.

The Barnardos network includes more than 40 project centres located in the heart of communities. It operates eight early years services, nineteen family support programmes, five teen parent programmes and four family welfare conference services. In addition, Barnardos provides some specialist programmes nationally such as counselling services dealing with childhood bereavement and post adoption, a guardian *ad litem* service representing children's interests in court proceedings and an information resource network for parents and childcare professionals.

Barnardos is committed to a *needs-led, outcomes-focused* approach in our delivery of services to children and families. At the heart of everything we do, we strive to achieve two outcomes for the children and young people:

- Increased emotional well-being
- Improved learning and development

We believe that if a child's learning and development, and his or her emotional well-being, is successfully and measurably improved through our work, then the child's ability to benefit from life opportunities and manage life challenges will be improved, and therefore the path of his or her life will be changed for the better.

For more information on Barnardos' work with children and families in Ireland today please visit www.barnardos.ie.

Believe in children

Barnardo's
Northern Ireland

Barnardo's Northern Ireland

Barnardo's NI is the largest charity working on behalf of children and young people in Northern Ireland. Our vision is that the lives of all children and young people should be free from poverty, abuse and discrimination. We aim to promote positive outcomes for all children in terms of their well-being, achievement and participation as young citizens.

Our focus is on those who are most disadvantaged, who are at risk, whose pathways in life have been fractured, and who face individual and collective adversities in their young lives that most of us will never encounter.

Barnardo's provides more than 40 local services in Northern Ireland. These services reach out, protect and support over 8,000 vulnerable and disadvantaged children, young people and their families in Northern Ireland every year. We also work in 150 schools in Northern Ireland, and have a network of 21 charity shops.

We offer support to children with disabilities; children who have been bereaved; children vulnerable to sexual exploitation; children of prisoners; young carers; young people upon leaving care; ethnic minority families; and families where there is domestic violence, addiction or mental health issues.

Our range of work includes professional fostering; counselling and therapeutic support; residential and respite care; assessment and family support; community outreach, parenting and early education programmes; training for employment; and disability inclusion services.

We use the knowledge gained from our direct work with children and young people to campaign for children's rights, bringing vital issues to the attention of the public and Northern Ireland Executive.

To find out more about Barnardo's NI or to help us fundraise, please contact us on +44 28 9067 2366 or visit www. barnardos.org.uk/northernireland.htm.

1

Introduction

Many years ago, while I was the governor of Mountjoy Prison, I was invited to speak to a group of parents of secondary school students. It is far too long ago for me to recall the exact occasion but I am pretty certain that the parents' association that invited me expected that I would focus on issues such as crime, drugs, underage drinking and other behaviour problems directly associated with teenagers. What I do remember is that the parents present were surprised that my talk focused more on parenting skills and the attitudes and expectations of parents than on issues like drugs, alcohol and behavioural problems. The reason for this is that, even back then, I was convinced that parents were by far the most significant influence in the lives of their children. I felt that if parents could get their act together as parents many of the conflicts and difficulties that arise between parents and their teenage children might never arise in the first place.

And so, over the last twenty or so years, I have developed a talk for parents that I call 'Parenting – The Challenges and the Rewards'. The content is based almost exclusively on my own experience as a parent for over thirty years and as a grandparent for the past two years. It captures my personal beliefs and philosophy on how we as parents can best help and support our children to grow and develop to their full potential. First off, I want to emphasise that I am very much an ordinary parent and I acquired most of my parenting knowledge and skills by trial and error and learning as I went along. Like the vast majority of parents, I had no real preparation for parenthood and received no training or direct help during the whole process. And so the purpose of this book is to share my personal philosophy on parenting based on my own experience as a parent.

Parenting Objectives

I often ask parents what the objective underpinning their parenting is; the answer to this should help guide them at all times. Many parents seldom, if ever, think about having parenting objectives. But I suggest that it is vital that all parents reflect on this and ask themselves, "What is my objective as a parent?" While I am sure that everyone will have different views and ideas, at the end of the day I think very few parents would disagree with me when I say that the key overall objective of parenting is to guide and nurture your child from babyhood through their childhood and teenage years to eventually becoming a mature, capable, independent, responsible and self-sufficient adult. How to do this is the difficult part, but the aim of this book is to guide you along this path. One useful way of looking at this is to regard your child's development as a process and, like all processes, there are many stages and elements along the way. Once you have decided on an overall long-term objective for your child's development broadly in line with the one I have outlined above, then every decision and action you take should be consistent and compatible with your overall objective. You should fully support and encourage your child to be as independent as possible from a very early age. Much of this urge and need to be independent will come naturally to your child and in many ways your job will be to provide encouragement. For example, encourage your child to hold their bottle, cup or spoon from a very early age. This is the first stage of gaining independence and even though it is a very small step it is significant when linked to your overall objective. If you ignore your child's efforts to be involved or you actively discourage their involvement your child will inevitably opt out and become totally dependent on you. Such an approach is completely in conflict with your overall objective. As they get older, asking your child what they like or prefer is another element in the overall process. Asking them what story they would like you to read them each night is a good starting point. Again, you are involving your child in decision-making and as your child grows and develops you should gradually give your child more and more control. Introduce the whole skill of negotiation to your child from an early age. Nothing very big is required at the beginning but the concept should be explained. Why? Because all our lives revolve around negotiations and the sooner your child understands this the better equipped they will be for school, for involvement in recreational activities, and so on.

Obviously, all of this must be done under your direct supervision at the beginning but your long-term objective is to help your child to become self-disciplined, responsible and accountable. As the parent you must remain in control and in the event of disagreement you must decide but you must always give a clear explanation of the basis of your decision. Autocratic decisions communicated in a dictatorial manner should be avoided at all cost because they do not involve your child in the decision-making process and when your child is not involved they are unlikely to be learning much about decision-making and, worse still, they will feel hurt and disrespected. As we discuss later in this book, your child will have to make big decisions from a young age around issues like smoking, drinking alcohol, sexual activities and drugs, and the best way to prepare them for this reality is to equip them with the knowledge, skills and confidence to make sound choices and decisions. In a nutshell, if you make all the decisions and totally dominate your child how on earth will your child be able to make sound decisions and good choices when you are not around to decide for them?

The Complexity of Parenting

Before teachers can teach in a classroom they must be qualified to do so and achieve a set standard of competency. Likewise, before people are allowed drive a car in a public place they must pass a driving test. But anyone, irrespective of their knowledge or ability, can take on the job of parenting. Despite the fact that over the past thirty or so years thinking has developed spectacularly in so many areas and formal qualifications and training are nowadays required for almost everything we do in life, it continues to amaze me how little status is given to the responsibility and complexity of parenting. I know of no other task that an adult will undertake in life that is as demanding, challenging, responsible, complicated and never-ending as parenting. Still, as a society, we operate on the basis that every adult has the capacity to be a 'good' parent and there appears to be a general assumption that all human beings have the necessary skills and knowledge to be capable, adequate and confident parents. Research shows that young parents are mostly influenced by the way they themselves were parented. The problem is that sometimes this influence was not very positive and as a result the negative consequences are simply passed on from generation to generation.

The reality is that most parents do their best and learn as they go along. But what is often forgotten is that when parents get it wrong there are usually very serious consequences for the children involved. There is a large amount of information out there on parenting, and parenting courses are available in many areas of the country. The internet, of course, also helps to make available a wide range of information on parenting. However, I am convinced that there is still a big vacuum and many parents struggle to cope with the demands of parenting at various times and stages in their children's development – in particular during the early teenage years. Most parents I have met have found the early teenage years of their children's development the most challenging and difficult to manage, and many were stressed out and at their wits' end trying to make sense of the whole process. Despite their best efforts, their relationship with their children often ended up strained and in some instances totally broken down.

Parenting in the wider context of society has changed over recent years. The structures of our society have changed and as a result the family- and community-based help and support available to young parents have been diminished. It is said that it takes a village to rear a child and I fully subscribe to this philosophy; the problem is that in most villages in modern Ireland that sense of community is no longer the norm and there is less and less social connection. The changes in the structure of the family unit in Ireland over recent years have been quite dramatic and the days of the stereotypical two-parent family are no longer the norm. Many children are now reared in lone-parent families; indeed, in some areas of urban Ireland up to 50 per cent of parents are single parents nowadays. There are also growing numbers of single-sex two-parent families, stepfamilies and 'blended' families. In addition, the old Irish tradition of the extended family having strong, close, supportive links with new parents is generally no longer the reality either. On the contrary, many young parents feel they are very much on their own and can rely on few links with their extended family or the local community. Added to this is the fact that in many cases both parents, either by personal choice or for financial reasons, work full-time outside the home; this brings added pressure, as it also does for working single parents.

The big question from a societal perspective is how best to deal with the issue of parenting and, above all, how to achieve the ideal balance between ensuring that, on the one hand, people are well prepared and equipped to take on the task of parenting and, on the other hand, there is not too much interference in the lives of young parents. Indeed, it is certainly an area that our educational system should have a significant role in. I have long believed that the Irish educational system is good at preparing and equipping most young people on how to make a living but is much less effective in preparing them on how to live.

I believe that parents with experience can help and support younger parents but it must be done in a non-interfering manner. Most of the young parents I have spoken with over the years usually resent interference, including that from their own parents. Nothing causes as much stress as grandparents or other immediate relatives or close personal friends offering unsolicited advice. While family members are full of good intentions, it seldom comes across like that to the young parents and the result is that they can often feel inadequate. Of course, the irony is that a few years later the same young parents who resented their family interfering in their early parenting exploits will themselves feel that they are now 'experts' in this whole area and will have no hesitation in offering advice to other young parents – and so the cycle continues. A great rule of thumb, therefore, is not to offer advice until you are asked.

One of the things I always say when I am speaking to a group of parents is that I have never met a perfect parent so far in my life and I do not believe I ever will. Accepting that all anyone can do is their best, that parenting is not an exact science and that there is no substitute for experience – these are all good starting points. Nearly every parent I have spoken with agreed that they were much more confident and relaxed when their second or subsequent children were born compared with their initial experience of parenting their first child. One of the advantages of getting older is that it is much easier to put life itself into proper perspective and to get your priorities right. Many of the issues that drove you mad and caused you stress in your early years as a parent soon become insignificant when you have to deal with real problems or challenges. I believe that it is very important to share this wisdom with young parents, since it often gives them reassurance and hope that they are doing okay and that reality could be much worse. For example, the things that troubled you when your child is well fade into the background if they become ill. In a nutshell, my aim when I am talking to parents is to share my own experiences with them with the benefit of hindsight, because hindsight is a wonderful thing.

One of the complexities of modern parenting is learning to deal with new aspects of today's culture, such as the rise of the internet. I would strongly recommend that all parents familiarise themselves with the potential dangers of the modern phenomenon of social media. Most parents are aware of the existence and dangers of cyberbullying, but may not know that there are many other potential dangers directly linked to social media websites which also place children and young people at serious risk. Unless you are an expert in the field, I would urge you to attend a talk on the potential dangers of social media and how you can help to protect your child. Indeed, this is something that parent associations at both primary and secondary school level could organise. The Gardaí will provide an expert if requested.

Finally, I always urge parents never to allow jealousy or boasting to become part of their parenting experience.

Jealousy can ruin your parenting experience and so you should nip it in the bud from day one. It often starts from the day the baby is born. Some parents continuously boast about their children and they get very jealous if another child of similar age is more advanced than their child, for example has more teeth, or is sitting up or walking earlier. This type of jealousy and competition often continues throughout the child's early years and into their teens and it can cause great tension and friction between parents, including close friends. My advice is to simply never go there.

Our Relationship with Our Children

As parents, our relationship with our children is one of the most complex challenges we face. It starts from almost day one in how we respond to our crying baby – do we leave the baby to cry or do we go to them immediately? "Am I too soft or am I too hard?" This is a key question that rumbles on for many years, often until our children leave home and sometimes even after this stage. So, what is the answer? The only advice I can give in this regard is that there is no ideal way and I am afraid a lot of the time it will come down to what you yourselves believe and your own interpretation of each situation.

The relationship between parents and a young child will be primarily dictated by the parents but it is a very significant period as the foundations for the future are already being laid. For example, a very domineering style of parenting is likely to make a child timid, nervous, insecure and lacking in self-confidence. On the other hand, a very laissez-faire style of parenting will provide no boundaries for the child and they will likely lack self-control, have no idea of how to relate to other children and adults, and will be very selfish. The ideal, I believe, is some place in the middle.

Of course in the early years the parents must be in control and make all the big decisions but I believe that a child should learn about choices and decision-making from an early age. I do not expect you to ask your four-year-old at 11 o'clock at night if they would like to go to bed now. But perhaps you could ask your child what bedtime story they would like. As your child grows and matures so should the relationship between you. This is something that some parents struggle with and they continue to treat a ten-year-old as if they are still five. This can cause great stress for parents and tension between themselves and their children.

As parents you should be aware that you have around twelve to fourteen years when your child wants you; after that you will be competing for their attention. During this period, your child admires you and look up to you; they want you to be present at most of their life events and they want your approval and support for everything they do. It is without doubt the most wonderful time in your parenting life and you should grab every single moment of it. This is the time to lay the foundation for the future. If you put in the effort during this period there is a good chance that when your child grows more independent, during their teenage years, they might still take some heed of you. I deal with this in more detail in Chapter 2.

Communication Is Key

In this book, I regularly return to the topic of the importance of communication and keeping an open dialogue with your children. Many of the problems discussed in this book would never arise if parents and their children spoke openly and freely about such issues, with both sides given the opportunity to have their say. There are hundreds of every-day issues that arise on which dialogue and negotiation with your child are appropriate from an early stage, perhaps from six or seven years of age onwards.

If you chat to your children all the time, then it will become a natural and normal part of your life and so when your child reaches teenage years it will continue to be very normal for them to chat with you; the topics of conversation will change but the dialogue will continue in a relaxed way. Listening is at the very hub of the whole communication process and, in particular, the need for parents to listen to their children throughout their childhood and beyond. I place great significance on the value of chatting with our children; we learn so much about our children when we chat with them. This is a key point to remember – your relationship with your child begins from day one and the early years are vital in laying the foundations for the years ahead. I believe the development of relationships, including a habit of good communication, starts from a very early stage in your child's life and you need to be aware that your child is learning from day one.

Parenting by Example

I would like you to visualise your children when they are young adults, say at the age of 25. At this stage they will most likely have left home and moved to a different part of the country or even somewhere abroad. Imagine one day meeting a complete stranger on the street or in the local supermarket and she approaches you and says, "I know your son. I work with him in New York." Naturally you enquire, "How is he doing? How's he getting on?" Now, reflect for a few seconds and think about what response from the stranger would make you feel happy and proud as a parent. The most popular responses are simple ones: "He's happy", "He's a kind person", "He's an honest person", "He's great craic", "He's a decent person, a lovely person", and so on. They are almost entirely about personal qualities and characteristics. No parent ever mentions materialistic things like, "I hope he's a millionaire." There is a very important message here for parents: the things that matter most are personal and human qualities rather than materialistic success. That is why it is so important to promote at every opportunity the benefits of human values and personal qualities. The following reflection highlights the need for parents to give example to their children by putting into practice in their day-to-day lives many of the values that they want their children to have.

Good Example
I'd rather see a lesson than to hear one any day,
I'd rather you'd walk with me than to merely show the way.
The eye's a better teacher and more willing than the ear,
And counsel is confusing but example's always clear.
The best of all the teachers are the ones who live the creed,
To see good put into action is what everybody needs.
I soon can learn to do it if you let me see it done,
I can see your hand in action but your tongue too fast may
   run.
And the counsel you are giving may be very fine and true,
But I'd rather get my lesson by observing what you do.
                                            – Anonymous

The maxim here is that there is no need to preach your virtues if you live by them. In other words, there is no need to tell people what you stand for and what you believe in if you live it every day. The example given by parents is one of the most powerful influences in the development of their children and it must be remembered that this can be for good or bad. If parents have good positive human values and principles, then it is very likely that their children will pick them up. Parents who are honest, truthful, kind, humble, forgiving, generous and compassionate are great role models for their children. Equally, parents who are the opposite of all those things will likely greatly influence their children to imitate them. I am sure you can think of examples in your own life of behaviours and attitudes being handed down from one generation to the next in a family. For example, if a child witnesses a parent being aggressive at home, the child will almost certainly grow to regard aggression as normal behaviour. If parents are dishonest and untruthful it is very likely that their children will also be so. Similarly, if parents are not afraid to stand up for what they believe it, their children will do the same.

During my talks to parents I usually ask the group if any of them would volunteer to be the adult role model for the young people in their local community. Unsurprisingly, so far no parent has volunteered. Could you imagine the pressure of such a role in a community, being an example for all young people day and night? Every time you slip up the young people will comment and remind you of your failings. The reality is that it is very difficult, if not impossible, to live by the high standards that many of us, as parents, expect of our children.

Sometimes as parents we can give out the message, 'Do as I say, not as I do.' I have personal experience of this. One of my best examples is when my daughter was learning to drive many years ago. I was acting as driving instructor one summer evening as we drove around the area in which we had lived for well over twenty years. With the learner's plate displayed we took off from outside our house. After travelling less than 300 metres I gave my first instruction. I shouted "Stop!" My daughter put her foot on the brake and we jerked to a stop. I pointed to a Stop sign located a few metres away. Not alone did I point it out, I also spelled out "S-T-O-P" just to make sure that she understood and that it registered. I went on to point out the significance of this sign, saying that every time you come to a Stop sign, you must stop, look left and right, and look left again to make sure that it is safe to enter onto a main road. Her first response was "Ah, thanks" and then just as we were about to move off she had a brainwave and said, "Hold on a minute. How come you never stop here?" If I stopped fully every time I drove through the junction in question there would be no need to tell my daughter about the importance of the Stop sign. Incidentally, my response was a typical father's reply when caught in a tricky situation, "Don't mind me."

The lesson here is to teach by example, not to preach what you do not practise yourself. One very appropriate observation I came across a few years ago was, 'Children insist upon behaving like their parents, despite the fact that one strives to teach them good manners.'

Parenting and the Home

The whole environment of the home has a major influence on a child's life and at times this is overlooked by parents. If I ask you to recall early memories of your home you will probably mention simple things that were very important to you and helped you feel safe and secure, at ease with yourself, and loved and respected. When I ask this question of parents, the most popular words mentioned are 'happy', 'fun', 'food', 'laughter' and 'friends visiting'. Now I acknowledge that for some people home was a very sad and unhappy place, a place where they were neglected or abused and injured. But I think it is fair to say that for the majority of people their childhood home is somewhere they think of with nostalgia. And one of the most amazing things is that, irrespective of how much time has passed since a person moved away from their original home, while their parents are still alive and living there the attraction of home never changes. When they return to their childhood home they

behave in the same way as when they lived there perma-
nently – that is the significance of home.

So creating a happy and relaxed home environment for
children is absolutely essential. You need to remember that
this is a key requirement and you should not get over-
obsessed with having your house spick and span all the
time. The day will come when you will not have to worry
about this. You will be living on your own and the house
will be immaculate at all times but it will also be a quiet and
sometimes lonely place. There might be a price to pay for
having a house of fun – it won't be the tidiest place in the
world but it will be a place that brings happiness and
contentment to the lives of your children. A home should
not be organised like a concentration camp, all rules and
regulations. It should be a place where your children's
friends are made welcome. I believe that this is very important and I encourage you to ensure that when a child comes
to visit your home they should be made welcome and
receive some hospitality, such as a drink, a biscuit or a
sweet – something that indicates that they are special
guests. And when these children grow up and become teenagers the very same principle should apply. The teenagers
should be made welcome and they too should be given
something when they visit – a cup of tea or coffee or a slice
of cake. Remember your own childhood and how much you
appreciated a little treat when you visited relations or
neighbours. These are the memories that last for a lifetime,
and you should replicate them for the next generation.
Another important observation is that you might be the
only person in that child's life who ever showed them such
kindness – one never knows. The one thing that is certain is
that kindness and generosity are always winners and are
always appreciated. Now I know exactly what it's like to
have six or seven children in the house on a wet Saturday
and it is very easy to lose your temper, but it is a wonderful

thing to see a group of children happy and enjoying themselves in your home.

Aims and Layout of this Book

While much of the main thrust of this book focuses on parenting pre-teens and teenagers, I want to stress that many of the suggestions and observations equally apply during the early years of childhood. Indeed, I would go so far as to say that all of the main principles should start from day one and should be the norm in your family. On that basis, much of the content of the book is relevant and appropriate for all parents irrespective of the age of their children. Parenting is an ongoing process and as parents we cannot dip in and out at various stages. It is now widely accepted that the early years of a child's life, especially the first three, are absolutely vital and greatly influence the future development of the child. All the principles outlined in this book are compatible with the early stages of both the child's and parents' development, as well as negotiating the teenage years. This advice equally applies to all non-parental guardians such as grandparents, aunts, uncles, older siblings, stepparents and foster parents.

The remainder of this book is structured as follows. Chapter 2 focuses on the importance of communication, which I have already briefly touched on, while Chapters 3 and 4 explore three very important aspects of developing a good relationship with your child – nurturing self-confidence, accepting your child, and supporting your child through the educational system.

In Chapters 5–9 I share my views on the complex phenomenon of bullying, underage drinking, the whole scourge of illegal drugs, trying to understand and prevent suicide, and, in particular, how parents might best handle these difficult issues.

Chapter 10 deals with the sensitive subject of educating your child on sex, porn, sexual crimes and relationships. It also addresses the issue of how to react if your child tells you that they are gay or bisexual. Chapter 11 looks at the importance of sport and other recreational activities in your child's life, while Chapter 12 focuses on the special role of fathers. Finally, Chapter 13 addresses the true measure of parenting success.

2

Communication

I regard communication as the most important function and responsibility of parenting. In the absence of good communication parenting is sure to suffer and in many cases fail. Indeed, the day that communication breaks down between parents and their children is the day that parents have a real problem. In many ways this is nothing but good common sense: if parents are unable to talk properly with their child, how can they contribute effectively to their development? So keeping the lines of communication open between you and your children must be your top priority as parents. And I am afraid in order to achieve this you will often have to bite your tongues, especially when your children reach the teenage years.

Communication is a two-way process, something that not all parents understand. The most important part of the communication process is listening and I would even go so far as to say that it is more important that parents listen to their children than the other way around. I am convinced that creating a safe, open, relaxed and easy-listening environment for children of all ages is one of the key tasks for all parents. Almost every problem or issue that will arise during a child's early years and well into their teens will have a far greater chance of being properly dealt with if the environment for listening is in place. Creating such a safe listening environment starts from a very early stage in your child's life. The remains of the old Irish tradition that children should be seen and not heard still linger today. Unfortunately it was this approach that allowed the many child abuse scandals that have rocked Irish society in recent years to continue for so long. A core finding of all the enquiries held into these scandals was that at the very heart of them was an alarming failure or refusal to listen to children when they complained. Equally significant was the discovery that many institutions had deliberately suppressed the voices and views of children in their care with the result that they were never given the opportunity to be heard. This was the main reason why their abuse and neglect never surfaced publicly for years, allowing the scandals to continue for decades.

The manner in which parents communicate with their children is significant from early in a child's life. By the age of two, children have already picked up many vibes and indications from their parents, positive and negative. Indeed, even before a child can talk they will be able to understand their parents' mannerisms and reactions to many of their behaviours and actions, so reacting in anger and frustration to a child's behaviour will leave a mark. For example, shouting at a small child indicates aggression and a lack of tolerance; aggressive behaviour will just encourage aggression in the child. What we do and how we do things are generally imitated by small children. The following little reflection is worth taking on board:

Children Learn What They Live

If children live with criticism, they learn to condemn.
If children live with hostility, they learn to fight.
If children live with fear, they learn to be apprehensive.
If children live with pity, they learn to feel sorry for themselves.
If children live with ridicule, they learn to feel shy.

If children live with jealousy, they learn to feel envy.
If children live with shame, they learn to feel guilty.
If children live with encouragement, they learn confidence.
If children live with tolerance, they learn patience.
If children live with praise, they learn appreciation.
If children live with acceptance, they learn to love.
If children live with approval, they learn to like themselves.
If children live with recognition, they learn it is good to have
   a goal.
If children live with sharing, they learn generosity.
If children live with honesty, they learn truthfulness.
If children live with fairness, they learn justice.
If children live with kindness and consideration, they learn
   respect.
If children live with security, they learn to have faith in them-
   selves and in those about them.
If children live with friendliness, they learn the world is a
   nice place in which to live.

– Dorothy Law Nolte

There are two vital pre-conditions to good communication which I believe should apply to all personal information shared by children with their parents, irrespective of their age. The first is that total confidentiality shall always apply to anything of a personal nature. As an adult, just reflect for a moment on what would stop you from sharing a personal, sensitive problem with another person, even a close friend or relation. I can safely bet that the one thing that would hold you back would be if you felt that person would not respect the confidentiality of the issue. If you believed that your personal information would become general knowledge in your neighbourhood or be shared with any other person without your permission you would certainly not confide it. The lack of confidentiality or breaching of confidentiality is one of the surest ways of destroying a personal relationship and undermining trust. The message here is simple and straightforward – all information of a personal nature shared by your child with you must always be treated with the utmost confidentiality. This principle should apply even when the child is very innocent and shares information that may seem to be very funny. Do not tell other family members or neighbours. If your child hears back from a third party the information shared with you they will find it very difficult to trust you again.

Also, no matter how amusing the information is, you should never make fun of your child or laugh or make little of the information. Remember that as far as your child is concerned this is a very important or serious matter and it should be treated as such by you. If your child is concerned about something that is just fantasy or an unlikely exaggeration, you should discuss this seriously with them and offer a clear explanation or clarification. Remember, they are children; they do not have the same understanding of the world and the likelihood of certain risks occurring as an adult. If your child feels you dealt with the issue well, they will continue to confide in you. If, on the other hand, they believe their concerns were treated as a big joke they will think twice before confiding in you in the future.

The second key pre-condition is to be totally non-judgemental. Again, as an adult you understand how a judgemental response, or even an indication that you are being judged, will immediately create a barrier. A look of surprise or shock can be enough to put a child or teenager off. Just imagine what it would feel like for a vulnerable person, such as a child or teenager, to be about to share a personal problem or worry with you only to get the sense that they are been judged. Once that signal has been received the child or teenager is surely going to make an excuse, change direction, close up and most likely never approach you with a personal issue again.

Obstacles to Honest Communication

When talking to parents I often tell this little story to get the message across about how a parent's reaction can influence honest communication with their child.

The Family China

A parent inherits a very valuable piece of china. It is over six generations old and at this stage is the family's pride and joy. Every neighbour and visitor to the home is aware of this treasure, which is placed proudly in the centre of the mantelpiece in the sitting room. A little baby is born and by the time he is mobile he is already well briefed on the value and importance of this family treasure. Naturally, as he gets bigger, he is told regularly not to go near it. But children being children, with their need to explore and investigate everything, the little three-year-old child climbs on a chair one day to have a closer look at the forbidden fruit. He lifts it off the mantelpiece to have a good look and it falls from his hands onto the floor, breaking into smithereens. Being a young and innocent child his immediate reaction is to pick it up and bring it out to the kitchen to show his parents what has happened.

So, how do his parents react? Many people in this situation would go ballistic. His parents dance around the kitchen screeching about the loss of the china piece and how they will never be able to replace it. Then their anger turns on the child. They remind him that he was told never to touch it or go near it, and after all that he still goes and breaks it. How could he? To rub salt in the wounds, every family member and neighbour who visits the house for months afterwards is bound to enquire after the missing china and the poor child is reminded time and time again about the trouble he has caused. He will never forget his first serious encounter with his parents; he has learned a lesson for life, but not the one we all think.

Some months later the parents decide to go into town and to replace the china with a lovely mantelpiece clock. The clock is now sitting pretty on the mantelpiece and as time passes by the china is slowly forgotten by the parents. The little child has been warned never to go near the clock. But as time passes his curiosity gets the better of him again and he gets up on the chair to have a closer look at the clock. He is attracted to the hands and begins to move them around. But the big hand breaks off and is lying in the palm of his hand. Now what is he going to do?

When I tell this story during a talk, most parents at this stage shout out "Hide it!" And of course that's exactly what he does; he sticks the hand back into the front of the clock, puts the chair back in place and gets away from the scene of the crime as quickly as possible. He fully remembers what happened when he reported his first misfortune; in fact, he will never forget that experience. The first time he was as honest as the day was long. He came out and told his parents exactly what had happened. He held up his hands and said, "I broke the china." But what did he learn from his first mistake? Believe it or not, he learned that honesty does not pay in that house. When he was truthful his parents made him feel miserable so of course he is not going to make the same 'mistake' again. Instead, he will hide the problem and lie his way out of it if necessary.

It is us adults who knock the honesty out of our children. However, the most important message in this little story is the long-term significance of how parents react to normal day-to-day events and incidents. In a nutshell, if parents rant and rave when they become aware of a mistake their child has made they are creating an environment that does not facilitate good communication, and in particular good listening. They are creating barriers that will eventually damage or even destroy communication between themselves and their children. So this brings me back to the necessity of creating safe listening conditions for our children.

In my view, during the first ten years or so of a child's life most of the responsibility for good communication rests with the parents because by the age of about ten most children will have learned that it is either safe to confide in their parents on all personal matters or they will be very selective on what to disclose or not. I believe this anonymous quotation illustrates how creating a safe environment for listening is one of the most important requirements in all human relationships: "To listen another person into a condition of disclosure is one of the greatest services we can bestow on another human being."

So as parents you have a choice – you can rant and rave and ruin communication between you and your children, or you can bite your tongue, keep your mouth shut at vital times and have good and open communication with your children. The choice is yours. The reason why children and particularly teenagers will not talk to their parents about personal and emotional issues is often because of hard evidence accumulated over a number of years when it was obvious to the child that either their parents were too embarrassed to talk openly about such issues, or they jumped in with solutions or harsh criticism, or they simply did not want to know.

One common reason for stunted communication between parents and their children is the generation gap. At some time during their parenting years most parents have heard comments from their children like, "What would you know about it?", "You don't understand", "That's ancient; it's very different nowadays", "You must have had a sad life" or "Ah, you should get a life." It is vital for parents to acknowledge the generation gap; it is there, and teenagers in particular believe it is real, so trying to force your beliefs on your children will simply not work. It is very hard for parents, especially young parents, to realise that most teenagers think that their parents were born in the dark ages and know absolutely nothing about modern life and their culture. Now, some of this is actually true and some of it is obviously not. Parents should know and understand that social culture continues to evolve and change at a rapid rate and even parents who were themselves teenagers only ten or fifteen years ago have little insight into their children's social culture. Many parents say to me, "But it's only a few years since I was like them and I thought my parents knew nothing." What they forget is that the world can change a lot in ten to fifteen years.

One of the main reasons why parents often respond in shock to something their teenager tells them is that they immediately see the dangers and they want to protect their children and prevent them getting into trouble and putting themselves at risk. Parents most likely remember suffering the pain of their mistakes and they are determined to share their wisdom with their children so they do not make the same mistakes. But do the children want to know? No, they don't. Did you want to listen to your own parents back when you were a young teenager? No, you didn't. Most parents I have met over the years were only too willing and happy to share their life wisdom with their children, but sadly their children simply did not want to know. They just went off and made the same mistakes and suffered similar pain to their parents, reaching the same place when they become parents ten or fifteen years later. It is a vicious circle, and it continues generation after generation.

The Value of Chatting

A basic reality is that we cannot force our wisdom on others, including our children, and we should begin the parenting journey by accepting this reality. As parents we tend to lecture far too much and listen far too little. I am confident that if we reversed the situation we would actually get to share some of our valuable wisdom; wisdom that we paid a big personal and emotional price for. One suggestion I always make to parents is to chat to their children from a very young age. Of course parents talk to their children all the time, but chatting is a particular style of communication insofar as it is always open-ended and two-way with absolutely no agenda. In my opinion we don't chat as much with our children as we might think. Much of our talk with our children is either probing or instructive. It is worthwhile reflecting on this for a moment. As parents we tend to ask a lot of questions: "Are you a good boy?", "How did you get on in school today?" or "Do you like school?" We tend to instruct: "Say you're sorry" or "Say thanks", and so on. Obviously all of this stuff is important and needs to be said. But chatting is quite different as it is a sharing process. It helps to build up trust and both sides get to know one another much better. Chatting can take place all the time, in any place. There is no need to plan it. Because there is no agenda, much of the advice you can't force on your children can be shared during chats. That is their value.

Watch how your children relate to older people like their grandparents. The dynamics of this communication are often different to the dynamics between parent and child. In many cases the child or teenager is relaxed and open when they are talking to their grandparents, since there is no parental agenda. I remember once talking to a fourteen-year-old about his grandmother and his summary was, "I love talking to her. She always listens. She treats me as an equal. She's interested in what I think and feel and she always knows what to say to me when I'm not sure of something." That is what chatting is all about – equality, sharing, listening, encouraging and caring. I believe that this approach cannot be started when the child is a teenager; it is much too late then. This should be a thing that starts at a very young age, from the time your child can talk, and it should be developed throughout childhood and the teenage years. I am confident that when you have a good track record in chatting with your children you will likely have a great insight into and knowledge of where they are at in their lives, and I would be surprised if any major issues or personal problems are suppressed by your child.

Chatting is a great way of discovering what your child enjoys or hates. What I have found over the years is that many parents do not realise the things their children hated during their childhood until much later in their lives. Equally, parents may not realise that it might be the simple things we do with our children every day that they really enjoy and appreciate. I often retell a story told to me by a friend many years ago about one of his early experiences of parenting. I tell this story because it remains a powerful example of the importance of the simple things we do with our children.

When putting his children to bed every night the last thing my friend used to do before turning off the light was to ask his children what their nicest memory of that day was. One evening he was putting his little four-year-old to bed and as usual he asked her, "Well, what was the highlight of today? What did you enjoy most of all?" The little girl thought for a few moments and then said, "Walking to school this morning holding your hand." I bet that most parents would never even dream that walking to school holding their parent's hand would be the highlight of a child's day. The beauty of it is that once you know the little things you do that matter to your child, you will just continue to do them.

Every single event in the day is an opportunity to chat: walking to school, walking in the park, going to the shops, driving to a match or sports training, eating dinner. You should also avail of every opportunity to listen to what your children are saying to each other, without interfering in their discussions. For example, when driving your children to school or watching them play, just get into the habit of listening. Ideally, you should be able to listen while pretending you have no interest whatsoever in what is being discussed. This is especially valuable as children get older, say around ten to twelve years, since at this stage they will not want their parents knowing what is going on. If a parent interrupts their conversation they will immediately change the subject or just nudge one another and whisper, "She's listening." The whole purpose of this type of listening is that it gives you a great insight into what is going on in your children's lives and the people and things that are their main influences. Irrespective of what you may hear during such conversations, you must never jump in and challenge or reprimand the children. Of course, this may need to be done, but later and perhaps in a different context. Interfering in your child's conversation with their friends will mean just one thing: they will stop talking in your presence, and you will lose a valuable tool for understanding your child.

Generally speaking, most parents have several opportunities every day to chat with their children up to around the beginning of secondary school. From then onwards it gets more complicated. For example, when your children are small, they will have breakfast before school, they will have lunch when they get home from school and they will be around the house most of the time until they go to bed, giving plenty of time and opportunity for you to chat and to listen. But many teenagers will not have an old-fashioned breakfast; they are much more likely to grab an apple or a yogurt as they run out the door in the morning. It is certainly most unlikely that they will sit chatting with you at the breakfast table. They will be in school at lunch time, and in the evenings they are likely to be coming and going all the time, doing sport or other recreational activities, or extra-curricular subjects. The opportunities to sit around casually and chat will therefore become more and more irregular. One thing that will not work in this situation is planning any type of formal gathering with your teenagers for family chats. Firstly, it won't happen. Secondly, it wouldn't work. And thirdly, if you actually got your teenage children all into the room I am sure you could just imagine the tension. You can bring a horse to water but you can't make him drink it, and I'm afraid it is the very same with teenagers – even if you got them to sit together in one room there is no guarantee that they would relax and chat. However, there is a crucial need to have at least one occasion every week where all the family can sit down and talk informally or in a normal routine situation. This does not have to be an exclusively family event; if friends of the parents or the teenagers are present that should not be a problem. In fact, it could be an advantage. The main consideration is to keep it an informal and casual occasion and to see your role as parents as mainly listening.

Personally I feel that Sunday lunch is one such routine and informal occasion. Food is at the centre of the occasion, and that normalises and relaxes the whole situation. An occasion where people can eat and chat at the same time is generally ideal. I encourage you to use an occasion like Sunday lunch to mostly listen to your teenagers as they chat amongst themselves. I know many parents who really cherish such occasions. Listening to their conversations will give you great insight into the culture in which your children live and how they relate to it and cope with it. The real challenge is not to interfere directly or to show open hostility or annoyance about what you are hearing. So if you discover that your fifteen-year-old daughter is an underage drinker, don't jump in and confront her. My advice is to just sit there and take it all in. Your response must be planned and thought out, and the timing of the intervention is equally important. Jumping in without any strategy is a recipe for disaster and is almost guaranteed to end up in tears. This does not mean that you as parents are soft on issues. The strategy is all about getting the best outcome. So, what is the best outcome if you discover that your teenager is an underage drinker? Well, the best outcome for the parents would be that the teenager stops drinking alcohol until she is eighteen years old and the best outcome for the teenager relates to how her parents deal with the issue.

Keeping the Lines of Communication Open

Before the main point is lost, it must be acknowledged that the best outcome of the chat in this scenario is that the parents became aware that their fifteen-year-daughter was an underage drinker. Prior to this the parents had no idea; they were totally oblivious to the situation. The point is, how can parents help their children if they do not have a clue what is happening in their lives? By getting this information the parents are now in a position to help and support their daughter. But one of the things they must ensure is that the vehicle that helped to provide the information – the chat during Sunday lunch – is fully protected at all costs; other-wise, it will soon become a thing of the past. The lunch might still take place but there will be no open and relaxed conversation among or with their teenagers. Indeed, they will likely never say anything at that table again.

Your strategy as parents must be to provide as many opportunities as possible to enable your children to commu-nicate with you and one of the main obstacles to that is likely to be you yourselves. Parents rarely do this deliberately but it happens because of how they react to the actions and behaviour of their children, or because of the children's perception of how their parents will respond in a given situation.

A number of factors contribute to a child's perception and beliefs of how their parents will react in certain situations. For example, parents' attitudes regarding misbehaviour will be communicated very clearly in how they react to the behaviour of other children. If they openly condemn other children and are tough and hard-hearted about particular issues or behaviours then naturally their own children will anticipate that their parents will respond in a similar way when it comes to them. Parents who rant and rave over minor issues certainly give their children the impression that getting into any trouble at all will not be tolerated in their family. Parents who are impatient or short-tempered will also make it difficult for their children to believe that, irrespective of what happens, they can still confide in them and look to them for help. Parents who just will not listen and who act as if they are always right definitely create barriers between themselves and their children. Parents who are living in the past and are trying to uphold ways of life that they grew up with will automatically give their children the impression that they are not open to or willing to engage with modern culture and societal changes. Parents who treat their children as inferiors and always speak down to them will make it impossible for their children to be open and confident that they will be supported and listened to when they are in difficulty. Parents who have very strong religious beliefs that are not shared by their children will make it awkward for their children to confide in them, especially regarding moral issues. Parents who never forgive or forget will give their children the impression that if they have done wrong they will not be forgiven.

These are just some of the attitudes and behaviours of parents that are likely to create serious barriers in the whole communication process with their children. Now, it is not all one-sided and not all the responsibility rests with the parents, but, as the adults, parents hold most of the responsibility. Also, they are the major influence in their children's lives for most of their lives and if barriers have been created much of the responsibility for this rests with parents. I am not suggesting that parents should not have their own values and standards for themselves and their children – of course I'm not. Parents are entitled to have whatever values and standards they wish, and to pass these on to their children, but the challenge lies in how they balance their values and standards with other important requirements of parenting. In a nutshell, would you prefer to have high personal values and standards and end up having no quality time with your teenage children and little or no communication with them? Would you prefer to be the last people your children would confide in should they ever have a personal crisis in their lives? I'm afraid that that is the most likely outcome if you do not control your reactions to confidences from your children, even if what they tell you is very serious.

As parents, you have a right to disagree with and disapprove of the behaviour of your teenagers and you have a right and a clear responsibility to communicate this to your children, but this should not be done at a time when your child or teenager is about to confide in you. Again, a lot depends on timing – when to respond and where. If the information you have received has upset or shocked you then the proper response at that particular time is just to be supportive of and caring to your child. Other than that the best thing to do is keep quiet and reflect on the whole situation. The natural tendency for most people to jump in immediately with little or no thought or strategy can often lead to a disastrous outcome. It is very difficult, if not impossible, to deal well with a sensitive situation when you are in shock or in anger, or when you are upset. Just take time out and come back to it when the time is right, which might not be for a day or so, depending on the circumstances. No matter how bad the problem seems at the time, it will be resolved over time if both sides are willing and committed to finding a solution. The legendary Sir Matt Busby, former manager of Manchester United, claimed that when he was confronted with any serious problem or crisis he always counted to ten before responding. Parents often feel under pressure to have all the answers and to be able to respond instantly to all family-based problems simply because they are the parents and the ones with the responsibility. My belief is that this is most unfair on themselves and it is far better to deal with a problem well by taking the time to react thoughtfully rather than rashly. Finally, I must point out that the approach I have outlined here is solely in relation to how parents should respond when a children confides in them or reveals something in their presence. However, parents are free to approach their children at any stage to raise an issue with them; the difference in this case being that it is the parents who are taking the initiative and not the child.

More about Listening

On the subject of listening I feel it is necessary to state that there is a big difference between listening and actually hearing. Many teenagers feel that their parents never really hear them. They say that their parents listen on occasion but they do not hear what is actually being said. Genuine listening and hearing can only take place if you give your full attention and concentration to what the other person is saying. You cannot listen properly if you are busy formulating a response in your mind. Listening is a wonderful and therapeutic activity. To properly listen to someone is also a clear demonstration that you value and respect that person. The great thing is that every person has the capacity to listen; they just need to take the time and have an interest in the person who is speaking. The following reflection provides a few useful guidelines for good attentive listening:

You Are Listening When ...

You come quietly into my private world and let me be

You really try to understand me when I do not make much sense

You don't take my problems from me but trust me to deal with them in my own way

You give me enough room to discover for myself why I feel upset and enough time to think for myself what is best

You allow me the dignity of making my own decisions even though you feel that I am wrong

You don't tell me that funny story you are just bursting to tell me

You allow me to make my experience the one that really matters

You accept my gratitude by telling me it is good to know that I have been helped

You realise that the hour I take from you leaves you a bit tired and drained

You grasp my point of view even when it goes against your sincere convictions

You accept me as I am – warts and all

You don't offer me religious solace when you sense I am not ready for it

You look at me, feel for me and really want to know me

You spend a short, valuable time with me and make me feel it is for ever

You hold back your desire to give me good advice

– Anonymous

From my perspective the above lines are all little gems, but two stand out for me. 'You accept me as I am – warts and all' is really the key one. If the listener feels superior or treats the other person as inferior then that attitude will come across and will undermine the whole listening process. The challenge is to listen as an equal. The second line that stands out for me is, 'You are listening when you hold back your desire to give me good advice.' When a person is in the process of confiding in another, the very last thing they want is a solution – someone else's solution. Just imagine you are in the middle of sharing a very difficult and sensitive personal problem and you are interrupted by the listener's solution or personal observation. It will instantly disrupt your train of thought, it will take the focus away from your story and it will make it difficult to pick up again where you left off. It takes the good from the whole listening session. A good listener just listens and hears as a first step. Suggestions and solutions can come later. It is claimed that if you listen attentively and properly you will know what to say – nothing. Just acknowledge that you have heard what is being said.

When You Become an Embarrassment to Your Teenager

Finally, there is one other obstacle to good communication between you and your teenager. It may be hard to visualise when you are the parent of a young child, but, believe me, the day will come when you will be an embarrassment to that child. It is always a bit of a shock when that day arrives, usually without any advance notice. Most parents of teenagers have their own experience of it. The day can come when the parents are not 'allowed' to have any opinions on anything, even simple things like the weather. You might offer an opinion – "Ah, it's a lovely evening" – but this will be ignored and your teenager will pull back the curtains to check for themselves. Gradually, you will realise that your opinions don't count anymore and over time you will concede defeat and stop giving your opinion. Eventually you will be treated like zombies with no views on anything. This can go on for a number of years and then out of the blue you will be asked for your opinion on something. You will be in total shock – just imagine having an opinion again!

This little reflection highlights the whole cycle in the relationship between parents and their children.

My Father When I Was

4 years old: *My daddy can do anything.*

5 years old: *My daddy knows a whole lot.*

6 years old: *My dad is smarter than your dad.*

8 years old: *My dad doesn't know exactly everything.*

10 years old: *In the olden days when my dad grew up, things were sure different.*

12 years old: *Oh, well, naturally Father doesn't know anything about that. He is too old to remember his childhood.*

14 years old: *Don't pay any attention to my father. He is so old-fashioned!*

21 years old: *Him? My Lord, he's hopelessly out of date.*

25 years old: *Dad knows a little about it, but then he should because he has been around so long.*

30 years old: *Maybe we should ask Dad what he thinks. After all, he's had a lot of experience.*

35 years old: *I'm not doing a single thing until I talk to Dad.*

40 years old: *I wonder how Dad would have handled it. He was so wise and had a world of experience.*

50 years old: *I'd give anything to have Dad here now so I could talk this over with him. Too bad I didn't appreciate how smart he was, I could have learned a lot from him.*

– Anonymous

I think most people can identify with the sequence above. It is very natural for your teenager to go through a period when their parents become the 'enemy', and so you should not worry unduly about this.

3

Nurturing Self-Confidence

For whatever reason, we Irish are pessimists almost by nature. By and large, we are far more likely to notice the things that are wrong and to highlight them than to notice all the things that are right. I believe most people will pick up on every single thing that is wrong or out of place at home and ignore or not even notice everything that is right. I am afraid it is very often the same when it comes to the way we deal with our children. We are far more interested in what they do wrong or fail in rather than what they do right. This simple story highlights this fact:

I was giving a talk to a group of parents one evening in Dublin and during my talk I emphasised the importance of positivity. I said that it was very important to affirm children of all ages and to always keep an eye out for the things that they do well. During the questions at the end of the evening a young mother stood up and said, "Well after what you said this evening about positivity I must confess that I must be the most negative person in Ireland." I responded by saying, "Not a chance, the competition is far too strong. But tell me, what did you do yesterday?" She said:

"Well my nine-year-old daughter ran in from school yesterday and said 'Mum, I did brilliant in English spellings today. I got nineteen out of twenty correct', and my first response was to say, 'And which one did you get wrong?' Then I did worse; I said to her, 'Show me that list' and my daughter took the list from her schoolbag. I stood over her like a sergeant major and went down through the list and when I came to the one she got wrong – she spelt the word 'still' s-t-i-l – I said to her 'It's a pity you didn't put in the second "l" as you would have gotten 100 per cent.'"

So whose interests had the mother at heart? Her own – she wanted to be able to tell all her neighbours and friends how great her daughter was, getting 100 per cent in a test. And what did the child learn? She learned that she could not spell, and she felt stupid and that she had disappointed her mother. Just imagine how she would have felt if her mother had given her a big hug and told her how clever she was. The little girl would have run around the house in delight, and then she would have gone straight up to her room to study new spellings so that in the next test she would do even better.

How many parents can identify with that mother? I certainly did.

Compliments, Criticism and Self-Confidence

Many of us parents are automatically attracted to the negative and fail to recognise the positive. Even when we receive a compliment we can find it difficult to accept it and often reject it. For example, you meet someone and compliment them by saying "How are you? You're looking well", and they reply, "Well I don't feel very well." When we get a few warm days we spend most of the time complaining about the heat or predicting that it won't last. It is actually amazing how negative and pessimistic many of us are, and this attitude can be very damaging when it comes to how we respond to our children.

I have little hesitation in saying that one of the best things a parent can give their child is self-confidence. The young person who has good self-confidence will take life in their stride and be well-equipped to cope with all the challenges and knockbacks that life will inflict on them. The confident person will fight back believing that they will overcome their difficulties and come out stronger at the other end. However, the person who lacks confidence will struggle when confronted with personal difficulties in their lives and many will opt out, believing that they are hopeless and are destined to be failures. For this reason it is vital that parents are ever-conscious of the significant role they play in their child's self-esteem and they should facilitate and actively support their children to develop positive personal confidence. We must remember that positivity, encouragement, praise and acknowledgement all contribute to the development of high self-esteem. Not surprisingly, criticism, negativity, rejection and always expecting more and more from our children directly undermines their confidence and self-esteem.

Children develop good self-confidence because they are affirmed and encouraged on an ongoing basis by parents and other significant people in their lives. For this reason it is very important that parents praise and affirm their children when they act responsibly, when they do their best and when they apply themselves to the best of their abilities. What is the difference between praise and affirmation? You praise your child by telling them how good they are and how proud you are of them, while affirming your child is linked more directly to the action they took – in affirming you say to your child something like, "I agree totally with you", "You handled that issue very well, well done", "I loved the way you painted the tree in that picture", "I love the sensitive way you spoke to that man" or "I wish I had your patience after seeing how you deal with that person." The difference is subtle but usually affirmation is done publicly rather than privately and focuses more on *how* your child does something rather than on what they do.

Offering criticism is one very damaging behaviour that we all do. I have never met a person who loves to be criticised; indeed all people hate criticism and most people actually resent it. If you want to help your child to improve or develop better skills or to change their behaviour you can do this in a positive way rather than by being negative and destructive. Instead of criticising what they do and how they do it, offer suggestions that might help them improve their performance or behaviour. If you want your child to develop and to feel positive about themselves then the best approach is to offer positive encouragement and to demonstrate a better way of doing something. And remember, as parents we should not always believe or insist that our way is the only way. Criticism makes us feel bad and inadequate; it saps away our self-confidence and it makes us feel useless. Praise, on the other hand, helps people to feel good and it generally gets the very best out of people. It was Mark Twain who said, "I can live for two months on a good compliment", and this is a good lesson to keep in mind.

As parents we should not confine our praise and affirmation to just measurable things like academic results, sporting success or community activities. All these things should be recognised but I also suggest that we should recognise and praise all the many personal qualities that our children display, for example when they are truthful, honest, kind, good-natured, sensitive, helpful or respectful to others. The reality is that we are more tuned into measurable achievements in our children's lives than to their human qualities and values. However, human qualities and values are just as, if not more, important and so it is essential to recognise the fact that a child is very truthful, for example. A comment such as "Well done and thanks for being so honest" will make your child feel good and will certainly encourage them to be honest in the future. It is much better to praise and encourage good acts and behaviour than to condemn bad behaviour.

Just as we must learn how to praise our children, we must learn how not to undermine their confidence. Below, I have identified a few things that I urge parents never to do.

Things Not to Say to Your Child

Never compare your child to any other child, either within the family or without. Every child is special and unique, and therefore any comparisons are unfair and usually turn out to be negative and destructive for the child. This occurs much more often than we might think. It can happen in the home, in the community, in schools, in sport and socially. Comments such as, "I wish you were as a good as your brother", "You must be good at sport because your brother was a great player", "How come you don't like music like your sister?" or "God, your sister was a pleasure to teach; I don't know where we got you" will all undermine your child's sense of self. It does not matter if the comparison aims to make the child feel good, such as, "You're much better at football than your brother" or "You are so much better in school than your older sister." I believe that comparisons are fundamentally unfair and likely to damage a child's self-confidence, and so they should be completely avoided.

Never resort to using put-downs, irrespective of your child's behaviour. Comments like "I didn't expect any better from you", "You must be one of the most stupid children in Ireland", "You are downright useless", "No wonder you have no friends; I'm not surprised", "You'll never be good for anything" or "You, a doctor? Cop on! You'll be lucky to get a job sweeping the roads" all severely undermine a person's self-confidence. One of the main factors leading to the use of put-downs is family arguments. I always advise parents not to argue with their children, especially with their teenagers. Parents usually respond with laughter and some surprise at this remark. They say things like "Ah you're not serious" or "That would be impossible in our house." However, I am serious. Arguments never solve anything; they usually damage relationships and very often when the argument gets heated hurtful comments are made by both sides. Never forget that it takes two people to argue. Also, as parents of teenagers know very well, they will seldom if ever win an argument with a teenager. A teenager's timing is usually deadly and their most cutting and hurtful comment will be made just as they are about to walk out the front door, prompting the parent to retaliate with their own put-down. It is at this point that the parent realises they have gone over the top and regrets saying such a hurtful thing but it is too late, the damage is done. Of course, I am not saying that the teenager is right to have a go at their parents, but equally two wrongs do not make a right. And it is the teenager who is far more likely to be damaged psychologically by hurtful comments. You should also remember that in an argument people are not listening to one another; they are far too busy thinking about what they are going to say next to get one up on the other side.

My advice is to discuss and debate any issues with your teenager but once there is any indication of things getting heated or turning into an argument you, as the adult, should call a halt. The approach is fairly simple – just say "No, we are not going to argue; we will come back to this again when we can talk in a calm and reasonable way." You will soon realise that with this approach problems will be solved more easily, relationships will be improved and the atmosphere in the home will be much more relaxed for everyone. All matters of discipline can be resolved with this approach. I now believe that even the most serious disciplinary matter can be dealt with without any long-winded and drawn-out rant. There is no need to spend a full hour ranting about a discipline issue that can be resolved far more effectively in one minute. Indeed, I believe that two or three sentences are more than adequate to deal with any teenage disciplinary issues. The first stage is to tell your child or teenager what the problem is and why you are unhappy with their behaviour. The second is to ask them for their side of the story. I absolutely believe that this should be done in every case. It is vital that you hear your child's perspective. Once this process is complete you should decide the penalty, if any. Again, one sentence is more than adequate – "You're grounded for two weeks" or "No television tonight" – and that should be the end of it. There is no need to bring the issue up again the next morning. It has been dealt with and now it is time to move on. Finally, you should remember that arguing late in the evening or at night usually ends up only upsetting you. You will likely spend most of the night thinking over what was said and will get up in the morning tired and still upset. Your teenager, on the other hand, will fall into the bed and have a great night's sleep.

Never deliberately or otherwise humiliate or embarrass your child or teenager. As parents we often do not realise that innocence is all part and parcel of growing up and not knowing something or not being able to fully comprehend an issue or experience is just a stage in the growing-up process. Of course we should give our children advice and support to help them understand the world, but we should always do it in a caring and sensitive manner. Some parents can make a joke of their child's innocence and talk to other adults about it in the presence of their child. We all know examples of young children saying something like, "Mammy, I have a pain in my tummy. Could there be a baby in there?" or "Is Daddy having a baby? He has a big tummy."

As parents we can find such comments amusing but we should remember that the little child is very serious and while we might think it is funny your child will not like you making fun of or joking about their innocence. Of course it is ok to laugh and enjoy your child's innocence but I suggest that you stop short of joking or making fun of it. This should never happen. Causing embarrassment for your child is once again undermining their confidence and making them feel stupid and foolish. The long-term consequence is likely to be that your child will disconnect and keep their views and feelings to themselves. You should just ask yourself how you feel when you are embarrassed.

Equally importantly, you should never set out to humiliate your child, irrespective of the circumstances. Rubbing their nose in it is sometimes put forward as a good and effective way to change the behaviour of a child. By this I mean, for example, if your son's school report is very poor and states that he does not concentrate and shows little interest in school or homework you tell all your family and neighbours and show them the report in his presence and slate his attitude, behaviour and lack of interest; you talk to his classmates and tell them how great they are and how you wish that your son was like them, again in his presence; and you show your family and friends his homework copies and point out the poor writing and misspellings, again in his presence. Or, if you are unhappy with the untidy nature of your daughter's bedroom you bring visiting family members or neighbours into her room while your daughter is there and proceed to highlight the untidiness of the room, pulling underwear from under the bed and making nasty comments like "A pig would not live like this" or "She is filthy." In my opinion this type of approach will do more damage than good and will leave your child feeling angry, humiliated and bitter. That is not a good outcome for either you or your child. Humiliating another person is always wrong and is nothing more than an abuse of power. Even when your child does something wrong and is caught in the act I still believe that the problem should be dealt with sensitively and with compassion. The objective must be to change your child's behaviour and not to damage them psychologically and emotionally. A parent can be very strict and firm when dealing with their child's misbehaviour, and must on occasion impose discipline and punishments, but never by humiliating their child. There is a huge difference between the two approaches.

Two Approaches to Discipline

This story illustrates two very different ways of approaching the same problem. Imagine your fifteen-year-old son damages the family computer by accidentally knocking a bottle of Coke, spilling it over the keyboard, but tries to cover it up and later denies all knowledge of the incident. You find out what happens when you bring the computer to a repair shop and they explain the cause of the damage.

With the hard-line, humiliating approach, you rush home in a rage and confront your son in front of your family and two of his friends who are visiting. Your challenge him immediately with accusations:

"What did you do to the computer? None of your lies now. I know what happened; you spilt Coke on the keyboard and ruined the computer. Why did you do that? Why? Do you think it is funny? And the worst part is that you are a liar, a rotten liar! Anyway I always knew you were a liar. This is not the first time – you told lies about your homework last week. You are a sly, conniving brat and I'm going to straighten you out. I have a good mind to give you a few slaps!"

Your son tries to explain: "I wanted to ..." but you interrupt immediately:

> "No more of that rubbish – 'I wanted to' – you wanted to tell me was it? Yeah, tell me lies! I want to hear no more lies from you. You deliberately ruined the computer and you will pay for it. It will be a long time again before you get any pocket money, and no more football either. And you can forget about school discos and summer holidays; you're grounded until I say so, do you understand that?"

The outcome of this approach is that your child was given no opportunity to explain what happened and why he did not own up. Actually he was terrified of your reaction and rightly so. He was humiliated in front of his friends, he has no idea how much he will have to pay, he will feel bitter about how he was treated and he is very unlikely to have learned anything positive about himself or how difficult incidents should be handled. And based on that experience he is very unlikely to own up the next time he does wrong and in all probability your relationship will be damaged or ruined.

The alternative is a much more relaxed and calm approach. This time you tackle the problem of the broken computer quite differently by talking calmly to your son:

> "Do you have any idea what happened to the computer? It's not working. Did anything happen to it or is it just past its sell-by-date? Look, if something happened just tell me and I'll get it fixed; it's not the end of the world. It could be worse – I broke it last year when I opened an email that had a virus."

If you take this approach I am confident that your son will tell you exactly what happened and why he did not own up immediately. If he does not and you take it to the repair shop where you are told that Coke was spilled on the keyboard, you plan your approach more carefully. When you arrive home and notice that your son has two of his friends visiting you say nothing. Later that evening, after tea, you ask your son to come for a walk as you want to chat with him about the computer. On the walk you proceed to tell him what the repairman found and point out that he is the only person in the house who drinks Coke:

> "Could you have spilled Coke on it or do you know what happened? Look, there is no point in denying it. It's no big deal, accidents happen. I know that you did not do it deliberately; I'm not going to eat you over it."

Once your son owns up and tells you what happened you say:

> "Well at last you have told the truth. You should have told me that at the beginning and it would have saved me a lot of trouble as I need not have taken it into the repair shop. There are two things now. First is the damage to the computer – you were told several times not to have open bottles of Coke close to the keyboard. Secondly, you told me lies and did not own up. You should have come straight down and told me what had happened but you decided otherwise and as a result I was blaming others for it. That is the worst part, causing me to be suspicious of others. I want you to promise me that you will never tell lies again. You are way above telling lies; it takes courage to tell the truth but it is always worth it in the end. Now you will have to pay towards the cost of replacing the keyboard, so I'm going to reduce your pocket money from €10 to €7 a week for the next ten weeks. That is €30, unless you want to pay it out of your savings – it's your choice. And for telling lies, you are not allowed to go to the school disco this month. Now, that's the end of it."

I am sure that your child will feel much better after being dealt with by this approach. He will likely feel bad for not telling the truth and owning up at the very start. He will realise that by telling lies he caused innocent members of his family to become suspects. He will have learned that dealing effectively with a difficult problem can be done in a calm and reasonable fashion. And he will have learned that when he does wrong he will have to pay for his mistake. But the best outcome is that your relationship with your son is intact.

Losing Your Temper

Finally, you should try never to lose your cool or get angry when dealing with your children. When I say this to parents they always look at me disbelievingly. However, I do believe that losing your cool as a parent or getting angry resolves nothing and usually only makes a bad situation much worse. If you think about it for a few seconds, can you recall any situation that was ever resolved satisfactorily while one or both parties in a dispute were agitated, angry, aggressive or in a rage? When we reflect on this question we have to accept that instead of helping, the anger only exacerbated the problem – and why? Simply because when we are angry we are not in full control of how we act. We all say things, often very hurtful comments, when we are angry that we would never say when we are relaxed and in control. The key message, therefore, is to avoid getting angry with your children and teenagers and to nurture their self-confidence.

4

Accepting Your Child and Choosing the Future

Accepting Your Child's Reality

I strongly believe that one of the most important require-ments for every parent is to completely accept the reality of their child. What I mean by this is that once your baby is born, you must accept them with no regrets or disappoint-ments and this must continue to be the situation throughout their life. This does not apply to babies born with serious illnesses or disabilities, in that it is very natural that you would not want your baby to have to cope with the difficul-ties, trauma and physical pain associated with serious illness or disability. This is very natural reaction by parents and completely understandable. What I am referring to is an entirely different set of circumstances. You must accept your baby as they are and with all of their natural features, abili-ties and personality, so you should not make comments like, "I had hoped it would be a boy/girl" or "He's got his father's nose, God help him." Later in your child's life, avoid comments than focus on characteristics, like, "I wish you were taller", "I wish you had more go in you; you are too easy-going", "God, you are no academic", "You have very awkward feet; all our family had small feet – I don't know where we got you" or "I wish you were like your older sister, she is so studious."

Trying to change your child can have negative consequences. Some parents can focus too much on their child's physical appearance. With girls this can mean worrying that they are not 'pretty' enough to get a 'good catch' later in life. This can lead to parents bringing their daughters to beauticians or doctors to have facial hair removed or a crooked nose fixed, or enforcing strict diets so their daughters are suitably slim. The result can be problems with body image and severe eating disorders. Similarly, with boys there may be pressure to build up muscle and to be a 'manly' man, leading to excessive weightlifting or even steroid abuse. Of course, if a child wants to improve their self-image through any of these (legal) measures that is perfectly fine, provided it is done with the consent and agreement of the child and that the parents are not forcing it on their children. However, too often it is the parent who is the one with the problem, and that is something that must be addressed.

As well as physical appearance, some parents can worry about their child's personality quirks and personal preferences. In Chapter 11 I explore the difficulties some parents have if their child does not enjoy sport as they do. This applies equally to other hobbies and interests, such as music, reading or science. As discussed in Chapter 11, your child's personal preferences must be accepted and respected. Trying to force an interest your child doesn't have on them will just create tension and lead them to hate even more the thing being pushed on them. On the other hand, your child may have an interest or hobby that you do not understand, such as an abiding fascination with Second World War history or building model airplanes. You should not discourage such behaviour or label it 'weird', but accept it is their hobby and try to gain an understanding and appreciation of it.

Your child's personality can also be radically different from yours. Your child might be quiet and shy where you are loud and boisterous. They may not enjoy going to large social engagements as you do, or vice versa. If this is the case, forcing them into social situations where they do not feel comfortable will not 'fix' the issue, it will just stress them out and create tension between you.

Your child is who he or she is and you must embrace him or her from day one; otherwise, you and your child will have a very miserable life – in your case always longing for your child to be someone they can never be, and in your child's case being constantly reminded of your disappointment in them and as a result growing up always having a sense of failure. Indeed, I would go so far as to say that accepting your child's reality is absolutely non-negotiable. If you think about it, there is nothing you can do to change who your child is, and trying to do so only puts pressure and stress on yourself. For many parents this is a difficult challenge. I have met literally thousands of parents who find it so hard to accept the reality of their children. How often do parents made comments like "Where did we get you?", "I wish you were like ...", "All the rest of our family were great at maths" or "Unfortunately, he's no good at sport"? The list is never-ending.

Accepting Your Child's Ability

Closely linked to accepting the reality of your child is knowing and accepting the *ability* of your child. Indeed, this is a vital issue, and one which causes many problems. Many a child's life was ruined because their parents had unrealistically high expectations of their abilities. Most parents are anxious about their child's academic abilities and, in my experience, many parents, often totally unintentionally, put huge pressure on their children to achieve more than they are capable of. I have no doubt that many parents have expectations that their child could never meet. The result is that the child's life is a constant struggle and they soon realise that they cannot measure up and so they believe that they are a total failure and childhood becomes an unhappy experience.

If a child is not reaching their parents' expectations in a given academic subject the response is often to send them to 'grinds'. The parent says, "Ah you'll have to get grinds to bring your maths up to scratch" and so the child is put under pressure to be good at maths. However the most likely outcome is that the child will grow to hate maths and to feel they are a failure, and the parents will just be frustrated. Of course, grinds have a place in our educational system and provided they are introduced to help your child reach their potential in a particular subject or to help your child to get a better understanding of a complex element of a subject like maths, science or a foreign language, they are excellent. It is when they are introduced for the wrong reason that they can do more harm than good. If your child has no gift or ability in a certain subject then you should accept that fact and move on. It is the parents who simple refuse to accept that their child is not academic or does not have great ability in a particular subject, and who consequently put pressure on their child to be something they are not capable of, who cause the most stress for teenagers.

Every parent should know the ability of their children and fully accept it. You should speak to your child's teacher on a regular basis and discuss your child's various abilities, likes, dislikes, interests and overall progress at school. By doing so, along with chatting to your child and helping with and observing homework, talking to coaches or mentors of any sports or activities your child is involved in and general observations, you will have a very good insight into your child's ability. You might not know the exact ability of your child in every subject and area – and you do not need to know – but what you do need is a good insight and with the help and support of your child's teachers you will have sufficient information to enable you to know the general ability and capacity of your child. Because of this, it is very important to have a good professional relationship with your child's teachers and you should pay attention to the teacher's views and assessments. Teachers will not always tell you what you want to hear, but it is what you need to know. Once you know your child's ability in any given area and accept it, this will guide your expectations. So if your child has a middle-of-the-road ability in maths then you must pitch your expectation at that level and help and support your child to maintain that level, but not expect that grinds or nagging will miraculously create an A-grade student.

Once you understand and accept the abilities of your child, your life will be far more relaxed and enjoyable and, most important of all, so will your child's life. If your child is average at an academic subject and they are getting results that reflect their true ability, then your child is achieving their full potential based on their ability and it is vital that your reaction reflects and accepts this. Comments like "Ah I know you're no good at maths" or "It's a pity you're not good at music" should never be made. When your child achieves their level of ability then they deserve the same praise and recognition as any other child, including the very high achievers. One must remember that the high flyer is also only achieving their ability. It is great to have a child who is a high achiever but parents should never be over the top with their praise, especially if there are other children in the family. Just imagine how a child who is not a high achiever will feel if the high achiever is always the centre of attention and lavished with praise. Children with average or low ability will soon realise that if ability is the only measurement that counts then they are doomed and their confidence and self-esteem will suffer greatly.

Many experts advise that rather than praising a child's intelligence – "You're so clever to get such high marks"

– you should praise the work your child put into their study – "You worked so hard on your French verbs and I'm really proud of you." Praising a child's intelligence can encourage them to coast because they believe they are naturally clever, whereas praising the work they put into something encourages them to continue to work hard. This also avoids the problem of unwittingly denigrating a less-intelligent but diligent child.

Following on from this, you should not claim any personal credit for the ability and talents of your child. They are gifts your child got at birth, and while of course you should be delighted for your child you should not take any credit. Talents and abilities are only good if your child makes the best use of them. I am aware of many people, young and old, who are some of the most talented people in Ireland but that talent and ability has not been developed or used by them and as a result they are missing out on enjoying and benefitting from their gifts. So the emphasis should be on how well your child uses and develops their talents rather than the talents themselves. I accept that it is very natural for you to compliment your child on being a beautiful singer, for example, but such a compliment should be balanced by reminding your child of how lucky they are to have such a beautiful voice. You should also occasionally remind your child of how fortunate they are to have the opportunity to develop their talents and gifts because many other equally talented children never get such opportunities. This applies especially to extracurricular activities like music, dancing and elocution classes. By having such discussions you will help your child to understand inequality and why the world is not always a fair and even playing pitch for every child.

Similarly, you should not boast if your child is blessed with outstanding ability. Of course you can and should be delighted for your child and feel proud of them, but it is important to keep everything in perspective and not go over the top. Parents often say to me, "But what is wrong with pushing our children to higher levels? We live in a competitive world and children must compete and learn to be winners." I have no problem with encouraging children to compete and to be competitive but what I am talking about is pushing a child beyond their ability, and this often happens because parents cannot accept that their children are not high flyers. The odds are that your child is an average child, because most children are – that's what average means. We must go back to one of my core measurements when trying to assess the success of parenting – a happy child and a happy childhood. A child who is being pushed way beyond their ability or a child whose parents have unrealistic expectations will not be a happy child and their childhood will be a stressful and destructive one.

What if My Child Is Not Achieving Their Potential?

Sometimes, however, your child is not reaching their potential. Parents sometimes ask "What do I do with a child who was great at English for many years but in the last year has gone backwards?" The issue here is not about ability; if your child has a certain ability in a subject and is failing to reach this level then you should talk with your child about the issue. However, it is very important not to jump to conclusions. Remember that there may be very good reasons why your child is not achieving their previous high standards. They might have a new teacher; there might be a problem in their life such as bullying, depression or drugs; or it might just be laziness. Your first step is to talk to your child, but not in a confrontational manner. Many parents respond by confronting their child rather than chatting about the issue. If there is a problem such as drugs or bullying your child will certainly not open up or confide in you if they believe you already have made up your mind about what is wrong.

The skill is to talk to your child with an open mind to try to discover what might be causing them to slacken off and underperform.

Do not start any conversation with a comment like "What is the matter with you?" or "What do you think you are doing?" These are all confrontational questions that will put your child on the defensive from the start. In this scenario, your child will likely deny any problem and the conversation can quickly escalate towards confrontation. A far better way is to lead into the problem or issue gradually. Begin by chatting about your child's life generally and how school is going. Talk about the teacher of the subject in question and how your child is getting on with that teacher; this will lead the conversation gradually to the central problem. Frame your query in an open manner: "I notice that you are not doing as well as you used to in Chemistry. Are you finding it very tough at present? I found Chemistry very difficult in fifth year." If the conversation is relaxed and low-key there is a much better chance that your child will open up, even if there is a problem like drugs or bullying. If you do not make progress with this approach you can get more specific and begin to ask more direct questions like "Is there anything or anyone distracting you or causing you trouble?" Or "What does your teacher feel about your results?" You do not have to get all the answers during the first chat; just reassure your child that you are concerned and that you only want what is best for them. As I highlight throughout this book, how easily this conversation proceeds depends on the type of relationship you have with your child. If you have regular chats covering a variety of issues, both general and personal, without any particular agenda, it is much more likely that your child will confide in you than if you only talk to them when there is a problem or an issue to resolve.

If you are satisfied that there are no underlying problems then it is quite reasonable to tell your child that they need to pull up their socks and work to the best of their ability. However, you should remember that as children get older and reach teenage years they can come under all kinds of pressure not to perform. Other children could be teasing them about being top of the class, being 'teacher's pet' or being a 'nerd', a 'geek' or a 'dork'. It is important to be aware that this type of teasing is often a reality for children and sadly parents are often the last to know about it. The ability of your child to cope with such teasing strongly depends on their level of maturity. The mature child will ignore the taunts but the immature or sensitive child can often find such teasing difficult and in order to be popular within the group or class will slacken off on study in order to be seen as one of the 'lads'. Maturity has often much less to do with age than many people imagine and much more to do with the child's overall development, experiences, exposure and ability. Some children are very slow to mature but they often catch up later in their teenage years.

The important thing to remember is that many issues can arise during your child's early years and it is very important to keep an eye and an ear out for any clues or indications of problems, such as a change in behaviour, mood, contentment or achievement, and then to chat to your child about what is happening in their life. In addition, you should constantly assure your child that some people appear to get satisfaction and enjoyment out of teasing and hurting others, that they are either sad or bad-minded people, and that the best policy is to ignore them. If this teasing develops into bullying, then you need to tackle that issue thoughtfully and strategically. The issue of bullying is explored more fully in Chapter 5.

The Key Message

The key point to take home is that you must accept fully each child's reality, you should know and accept your child's ability, you should set your expectations for your children based exclusively on their ability and once they are reaching their ability you should give them the same recognition as any other child. Highly talented and gifted children should not be given over-the-top praise, especially when there are other children in the family and in earshot. And, finally, children should be praised for the work they put into their studies, not for their intelligence or perceived intelligence.

Choosing School Subjects

When it comes to choosing the subjects to study for the Leaving Certificate, I want to make an important point. Many teenagers are encouraged to select subjects that will enable them to apply for a particular course at university. However, I am quite confident that most children at fifteen or sixteen years of age have very little certainty regarding what career they want to pursue and many will change their minds several times even before they come to the stage of filling out the CAO form. Some of you will remember the late Christina Murphy; she was a teacher for many years and also the education correspondent for the *Irish Times*. In 1995 I attended a talk she delivered to parents and students who were about to start fifth year in secondary school. During the talk she offered the following advice regarding the selection of subjects for the Leaving Certificate:

"Don't be targeting any particular third-level course at this stage because by the time you're ready to start college you might have changed your mind, so keep your options open and study the subjects that will cover you to apply for all the most important courses. Irish, English and Maths are compulsory so get on with them, you have no choice. Study a foreign language and do at least one science subject. Those five subjects will ensure that you will have total flexibility when it comes to selecting third-level courses. Now pick one subject that you really love and enjoy. Just forget the whole points thing when selecting this subject. On days that you are fed up you'll be able to say, 'Ah well, at least I have my favourite subject afterwards' and that subject will pull you through many difficult days."

I cannot think of any better advice. You should urge your teenagers to keep their options open as much as possible when they are deciding on the subjects to study for their Leaving Cert.

I want to emphasise Christina Murphy's advice about selecting one subject that the child really enjoys. For example, someone who loves music but might never get high marks in examinations should select Music as a subject simply because they love it. For some students the subject they most enjoy will be one in the list of five and if so that's great. For others it will not be. As with playing sports, the main issue is enjoyment; second-level education is very competitive mainly because of the need to gain sufficient points for a person's chosen third-level course. As a result, much of the enjoyment is taken out of education and anything that helps to redress this is worth trying. You should emphasise this when you are talking with your teenagers about selecting subjects for their Leaving Certificate.

The CAO Application Form

In more recent times, especially since the economic recession, I have met numerous parents who are very stressed because of conflict between themselves and their children regarding filling out the CAO application form. The core issue is nearly always the same – the parents feel or indeed have decided that their child is making a bad career choice and they will not allow their child to apply for the course of their choice. I hear comments like, "I'll be paying for her to go to college and there's no way that she is doing that course", "He is selecting a course that has very low points because he just does not want to put the effort into his studies to get higher points for a better course", "There are no jobs in that field any more so it would be a waste of time" or "I didn't send him to a private school to do a Mickey Mouse course in university." Worse still, more and more parents are actually making course choices for their children. To say that this approach is disastrous is a severe understatement.

One issue that causes great difficulties for some parents is the connection they make between various courses and the number of CAO points required. There are two quite different issues arising here. The first is that some parents believe that just because the points requirement for a course is low then it automatically follows that the course is not much good. However, this is simply not true and if this is the course that your child prefers you must accept it. I also know of parents who have a snobbish attitude to education and when their child indicates that they want to do, for example, an Arts degree at third level the parents' response is "We did not send you to a good secondary school for you to do an Arts degree." This is an outrageous attitude and should never be considered as a factor in your child's choice of a third-level course. The second issue is when a teenager selects their preferred third-level course and their parents believe they only selected the course because it has a low points requirement and that they are lazy and want to doss during Leaving Cert year. Again, however, very often the child genuinely prefers that course and you should accept your child's decision unless you have concrete evidence to the contrary. I emphasise here, once again, the importance of having regular chats with your child; if you are having ongoing open dialogue with your child all these issues will be discussed and debated long before the time comes to fill out the CAO application form. You will have a very good knowledge of your child's interests and the career path they have in mind so the chance of surprises will be slim. Most problems in relation to the filling out of the CAO application form arise because there has not been adequate dialogue between parents and teenager prior to this. Early and open discussion with your child will prevent problems and disagreements arising in the first place.

I have emphasised many times in this book that the aim of parents should be to seek the agreement and consent of their children as much as possible. This approach is based on my belief that anything that is forced on a child is almost certain to be rejected by them at the first opportunity. On the other hand, most things that a child enjoys during their childhood and teenage years are very likely to be the things that they will continue to love and treasure for the rest of their life. Parents who believe that just because they are paying for their child's education they are entitled to decide their child's future need to cop on, urgently. Of course you should discuss such matters with your teenagers and give your advice and opinions on courses at third level, but you must allow your teenager to make the final decision, irrespective of how you feel. Any other approach will be high risk and will most likely result in your child either dropping out of college altogether or remaining in college but hating every minute of it. And when their life runs into any difficulty in the future you will certainly be given the blame. It is also important to remember that at the time of applying for third-level college places most children will be seventeen or eighteen years old. In other words, they will be almost, if not already, an adult. At that age they must accept full responsibility for their lives and for the decisions they make, including selecting their courses at third level.

So when it comes time for your child to fill out their CAO application form, I would urge you to be sensible and to accept that it is your child's life and their happiness that is being decided. You may know better than your children what work opportunities are available at present, but if your child is not interested in or is opposed to studying in that field then you must fully accept their wishes. I have no hesitation in saying that it is much better to have your adult child working in a job that they enjoy rather than being unhappy working in what you might regard as a 'better class' job.

Another point worth considering is that, while your teenager may have some specific career ambitions and will select third-level courses to assist those ambitions, it is very possible that they will subsequently change their minds and end up in a completely different career. Sometimes this is because the career they had in mind was not really for them, they discovered that they were not suitable for that type of work or, as they grew older and more mature, they just changed their mind and decided to go a different direction. I believe that many people end up in a particular job or career as much by chance as by desire. While it is great that your child plans for the future by selecting the right third-level courses to facilitate their chosen career path, life does not always work out as planned. But, provided they have all the basics right, they will be in a good position to respond to any career opportunity that arises out of the blue. Life can be unpredictable at the best of times and it is very important that your child is prepared for such unpredictability, especially when it comes to careers and work opportunities.

While you should not dictate your child's college course, you can provide positive support in helping them to decide how to fill out their CAO form. Many secondary schools have a career guidance counsellor on their staff and your child should certainly consult with this teacher. I am aware that currently career guidance posts are coming under pressure to be retained in many secondary schools and this service might not now be available to your child. If that is the situation it may be a good idea to talk to your child about having a session with a private career guidance counsellor. Some young people are very clear on the career they want to pursue while others have simply no idea and in such cases it is definitely worthwhile visiting a career guidance counsellor, who can run some tests and help your child to understand where their strengths and interests lie.

One delicate issue to be aware of is that on occasion a young person will wish to apply for a course that requires very high points and the reality is that they have no realistic chance of getting the required points in the Leaving Certificate. This is a very sensitive issue for parents and you should discuss it carefully with your child. It is absolutely essential that your child gives a lot of thought to their second, third and fourth choices. Many teenagers put all their eggs in one basket and if they do not get the points they need for their first choice they are completely thrown and it is only then that they realise the importance of their second and third choices. And because they were so focused on their first choice they often overlook the fact that their second choice might require an aptitude test in addition to the points required. But the aptitude test is normally scheduled months prior to the Leaving Certificate results becoming available, so their second choice is also gone.

One final point in this area – you should be prepared for the disappointment and, in some cases, the devastation, of your child when the Leaving Certificate results come out if they are substantially below your child's expectations and perhaps yours also. When this happens your child will need your full support. It is not the end of the world by any stretch of the imagination but your child will not see it that way. The very last thing your child needs now is a disappointed or angry parent; this is an occasion where your unconditional love is required.

5

Bullying

There is no doubt whatsoever that bullying has become a huge issue for many people in modern Irish society. Obviously bullying has always occurred but I think it is fair and accurate to say that in the recent past it has become a major issue throughout society and at every level. Much of this is due to more openness nowadays and also due to much more focus being placed on this despicable activity. In addition, with the developments in technology, the phenomenon of cyberbullying is now widespread and unfortunately it has become very difficult to identify the culprits and to control and eradicate this horrible activity. In this chapter I am going to focus on the elements of bullying that concern parents and children. The whole bullying scene is much too large and complex an issue to be adequately deal with in this book. But I will clarify a few things to help you identify what constitutes bullying and what to look out for in relation to your own children. It is also important to be aware that a child could be a victim of bullying in one situation and be the bully in another situation.

I want to stress that bullying is a non-gendered activity and is most certainly not confined to aggressive males. Actually, girls are just as likely to be involved in bullying as boys. It is important to realise that bullying can involve very young children, say as young as seven or eight years of age; many suffer greatly as a result and they are often too young to know and understand what is happening. Indeed, small children can be extremely cruel to one another and, for example, refuse to allow a child to play with a group of other children of the same age – such behaviour over time could constitute bullying. I am not suggesting that such young children are consciously involved in bullying but many of the elements of what constitutes bullying are present and without correction the child could go on to be a bully. So the message is that bullying can involve any age group, any social class, boys and girls, and a child can be a bully or a victim of bullying, even at the same time. You should therefore keep an open mind to the possibility that one of your children could be involved in bullying or be a victim of bullying.

What Is Bullying?

There are a number of definitions of what constitutes bullying and the following is generally accepted as an accurate and reasonable definition: bullying is offensive, abusive, intimidating, malicious or insulting behaviour, or abuse of power conducted by an individual or group against others, which makes the victims feel upset, threatened, humiliated or vulnerable, which undermines their self-confidence and which may cause them to suffer stress. Bullying is a behaviour which is persistent, systematic and ongoing. It is very important not to confuse bullying with other behaviours. Some people can claim that they were bullied and when the allegation is investigated it turns out that while they were involved in a serious disagreement and an abusive argument, it was a once-off incident and so did not constitute an act of bullying. The Department of Education and Skills describes bullying as 'repeated aggression, verbal, psychological or physical, used by an individual or groups against others'.

The following are some of the behaviours that can be characterised as bullying:

- Manipulation of a person's good reputation by rumour, gossip, ridicule or innuendo
- Preventing a person from speaking by using aggressive and/or obscene language
- Social exclusion or isolation
- Intimidation
- Physical abuse or threats of abuse
- Aggressive behaviour or shouting, often over quite unimportant matters
- Swearing or other forms of demeaning name calling
- Insulting or unnecessarily commenting on the appearance of another person
- Making a person's opinions and beliefs the butt of jokes or uncomplimentary remarks
- Physically attacking, threatening to attack or acting in a menacing way towards another person
- Deliberately ignoring or excluding a person on a persistent basis
- Unwarranted or disproportionate criticism of a person's work which is not supported by facts

The above examples are very broad and cover the most frequently identified forms of bullying. Obviously in the case of children some of these examples don't apply or when they do they may be a watered-down version, but the general principles apply. However, parents should know that children can participate in many forms of bullying; I provide more examples and details below.

One of the biggest myths that still exist in many people's minds is that bullying normally has a physical element. Nothing could be further from the truth, and indeed if it was true it would be much easier to deal with it because any physical abuse or injury inflicted on another person is an assault and can be dealt with as a criminal offence through the courts system. It is my experience that most bullying incidents do not involve a serious physical element. The reality is that most of the damage caused by bullying is either mental, such as depression, anxiety and paranoia, or psychological, such as the erosion of self-esteem, self-confidence and self-belief. In addition, teenagers who are experiencing bullying will often develop feelings of guilt – blaming themselves for the behaviour of the bully, and so on. As well as this, the resultant stress of being bullied will damage a person's general health and well-being. Unsurprisingly, it is very difficult to measure and prove the health and psychological damage caused by bullying and many people who have experienced bullying, irrespective of their age or social status, find the challenge of providing proof a major problem and are often frustrated in their fight for justice. That is why bullying is so difficult to eliminate and why many bullies get away with it. However, this must not be interpreted as saying that there is little point in pursuing a complaint of bullying. All bullying incidents should be fully responded to and you should be proactive in supporting and protecting your children when they are the targets of bullying. Just be aware that confronting and eliminating bullying can be a challenging and difficult undertaking requiring a lot of planning and plenty of patience.

Where does bullying occur? The answer is any place where people live or assemble. Bullying is not confined to any particular area or location, such as schools, clubs or workplaces.

Consequences of Bullying

What are the most negative and damaging consequences of bullying? Bullying can:

* Damage a victim's health physically and mentally, leading to headaches, migraines, tiredness, exhaustion and constant fatigue
* Cause high levels of stress and anxiety
* Cause sleeplessness and nightmares
* Result in the victim obsessing about the bully
* Lead to the victim being fearful and always on edge
* Damage and undermine self-confidence and self-esteem
* Often be a major contributory factor in suicides

Bullying v Teasing

It is important that we do not confuse bullying with what could be classified as the type of normal banter and good-humoured slagging that frequently occurs between children and which is very much part-and-parcel of growing up. But what is vital is that humour, banter, teasing and slagging must not venture into sustained personal attacks or the humiliation of individuals. That over-used excuse put for-ward by many young people – "Ah we were only messing" – is not acceptable. A good rule of thumb is if the same child is at the receiving end of consistent slagging and feels hurt or vulnerable as a result then that behaviour can be classified as bullying.

Not all slagging and teasing is bullying, but quite often it becomes bullying when it involves nasty personal comments and it is sustained over a period of time. A once-off incident of slagging or teasing is not bullying but if it goes on for a period of time then it certainly can be classified as bullying; to clarify what I consider a 'period of time' – it could be as short a period as two or three days. A good rule of thumb is if the slagging is returned to on a regular basis over a short period and is a sustained attack on the individual then it moves from the slagging or teasing stage to bullying. I believe that slagging is much too freely accepted in Ireland as harmless and only 'a bit of craic' when in actual fact it is hurtful and quite damaging for the individual who is being subjected to it. You should also remember that during early teenage years children are going through puberty and as a result they are much more vulnerable to this type of abuse – and that's what it is, abuse.

Common Forms of Bullying

Bullying can take numerous forms and below I discuss some common examples. One form of bullying used by both boys and girls is to make negative comments about the physical appearance of a person or the nationality of the person. This is *not* acceptable. Of course, any comments of a racist nature are completely unacceptable.

Research shows that generally speaking boys and girls bully in very different ways. Boys use more aggressive behaviour like pushing, kicking, poking, knocking over or jumping on a victim. They often intimidate a victim by threatening to be physical. Boys bully victims by damaging their personal property like clothing, school books, bicycles and mobile phones. They often force their victims to hand over their pocket money, to steal alcohol from their home or to do homework for the bully. Another often-used tactic is teasing a boy about his sisters or mother with sexual innuendos. A group of boys hold a discussion about another boy's mother or sister and pretend that they had a sexual experience with them; they speak and laugh about "what she was like" or "how good the sex was" with his mother or sister. This can be very upsetting for the boy in question. However, a related problem is that if the individual reacts to this 'slagging' or to the name-calling discussed below they will become even a bigger target of bullying. So the child soon finds himself in an impossible situation and life becomes hell on earth.

Finally, an extremely common form of bullying among boys is to slag victims about their sexuality and masculinity. In the context of bullying the terms 'gay', 'queer' and 'bent' are used deliberately to hurt, upset and ridicule the victim. The reality is that the whole tone and language used by the bully and, above all, the attitude it conveys is very hurtful to all victims irrespective of their sexuality. Bullies will say to a teenager "You're gay" or "You're queer" and quite often a whole class of boys and girls will find it very amusing and openly laugh at the individual, undermining their sense of self. It is very important in addressing this issue that you do not confuse the sensitive issue of sexuality with some of the terms used by bullies against their victims. In talking to your children about such bullying behaviour you must assert firmly that the sexual orientation of an individual is a funda-mental human right and under no circumstances is it acceptable that they should be subjected to nasty comments or slagging about their sexuality or perceived sexuality. You need to reaffirm time and time again that people who are gay, young and old, are normal human beings and their sexual orientation is part of who they are. I think it is fair to say that during early teenage years the issue of sexuality is particularly sensitive for both boys and girls and parents should be very conscious of this reality in all their discus-sions with their teenagers. Under no circumstances should you ever involve yourself in conversation with your chil-dren or in their hearing that mocks or laughs at the sexuality of others or sexuality in general. Indeed, in my opinion, sexuality should never be discussed in this manner. The issue of sexuality is explored in more detail in Chapter 10.

Just as boys frequently call the sexuality of their victims into question, so they also question their masculinity by name-calling. This is not what you might expect as the normal sort of name-calling; this is when girl's names are used to slag an individual. So a boy is called 'Mary' or 'Susie' or 'Rosie', and this will be most annoying and upsetting for the individual. Again, this can have devastating consequences by undermining their self-confidence or, if they respond, by creating an even stronger backlash.

Girls, on the other hand, usually bully in a quiet and covert manner. They will whisper to their friend about their victim when the victim is within hearing distance. They will disclose personal information previously gained in confidence from the victim and this will often hurt and humiliate the victim. Girls will spread gossip and malicious rumours about their victims and refer to them as 'sluts'. They will manipulate the friends of victims and break up their relationships. They will exclude victims by ignoring their views and inputs and they will jeer and laugh at them and make fun of them in front of other girls. Girls will slag their victims about boyfriends, if the victim is in a relationship, or for not having a boyfriend as the case may be. Girls will focus on the style of clothing worn by their victims and make them feel uncomfortable. Girls are known to write horrible notes on the copybooks of victims in schools or to write notes and place them in the school lockers of victims.

Of course, there will be some crossover but generally speaking boys and girls use different bullying tactics and methods. The one common denominator is in the area of cyberbullying; both boys and girls use this form of bullying.

Cyberbullying

In more recent times a new and very sinister development called 'cyberbullying' has arrived on the scene and this continues to cause horrible consequences for vulnerable young people. Cyberbullying is when the internet, mobile phones or other technology or devices are used to send or post messages or images intended to hurt, damage or embarrass another person. Almost any website or digital technology can be used to bully, and one of the most difficult aspects of cyberbullying is that so much online activity occurs anonymously. Typical cyberbullying behaviour includes sending threatening or hateful messages and images via text, email, and in comments on sites such as Facebook, Ask.fm and YouTube; impersonating another person on a social networking or other site and posting offensive or inappropriate material in the victim's name; and sending nude or degrading images of a person to friends, where they can quickly spread through the peer group.

We live in an age of technology and there is little, if anything, we as adults can do to control or reduce its impact but children must learn that they must be held responsible for their actions and this definitely includes their behaviour on the internet. The big problem with this form of bullying is that it can operate 24 hours a day, 7 days a week. It is unrelenting and pervasive and there is no hiding place from it except to disconnect from the internet or not visit particular websites on which abuse occurs. However, young people are anxious to know what is being said about them, so they find this difficult to do, and it is also not considered 'cool' to disconnect from social networking. The extra dimension in this type of bullying is that the comments remain forever in cyberspace and the audience is widespread. The remarks made are often very vicious and extremely cruel and there are few restrictions on what can be posted. While most website will have a 'report abuse' button and have the power to remove hateful or abusive comments or to block the offender from the website, the problem is that it can often take time – too much time – for a moderator to respond to complaints, if one is made; they may not take action because they feel this would infringe on the free speech rights of the bully; or the bully can simply create more accounts using different names and email addresses in order to continue their campaign. The 'report abuse' button can also be used as a cyberbullying tool against a victim, by portraying them as the aggressor. The fact that the bully is anonymous online creates a safety net for them and leaves the victim to wonder who is saying such horrible things. Within a few seconds literally thousands of people have access to the hurtful comments and the victim has no immediate comeback. If they do respond with comments of their own this can just encourage the bullies to continue or even ramp up their campaign.

You can readily see how this form of bullying has the potential to destroy the life of a young person. For most of us it is difficult to understand why children subjected to this type of bullying do not confide in their parents, but, as I discuss below, the culture is to not report it and not discuss it with adults. This culture must be the number one target when adults are wondering what they should do to help. This culture of secrecy must be broken and this can only be done with the agreement and support of young people. I believe that parents, teachers, youth leaders, school chaplains and children must all work together to break this scourge, and that is what it is. In addition, governments must urgently legislate to control and outlaw some elements of this horrible practice. As a society we cannot stand idly by while so many young children suffer ongoing abuse with no controls or accountability for those who are responsible. A second reason for not reporting cyberbullying is that perhaps some teenagers are afraid their parents will 'freak out' or will ban them from using certain sites or using the internet altogether, or remove their mobile phone.

If your child is suffering from cyberbullying there are some practical things you can do to counteract the problem.

If you contact your internet service provider it may be possible to track the bully to the computer they use, through their IP address. You can block particular phone numbers, email addresses, accounts on Facebook, etc. so your child does not receive messages from them – not all cyberbullying in anonymous. Use the 'report abuse' button if one is available on the website on which the abuse is occurring. Report the problem to the Gardaí, taking care to record the details of the abuse, just as with offline bullying. If the problem is not resolved you can also change your child's phone number, email address and online identity and only give these details out to close friends.

You should talk to your children, from seven or eight years of age onwards, about the dangers of the internet and of cyberbullying. Your child should be made aware that putting any damaging information, gossip or material about or affecting another person on the internet, on websites such as Facebook or Twitter, or distributing them by text or email, is completely unacceptable. Chat to your children regularly about the consequences and serious damage such actions can have on other people. You should help your child to understand that by using technology their audience is potentially huge and they will not have control over the information they distribute and also the consequences arising as a result of other people commenting on, adding to or manipulating their original message.

As part of this discussion, you should also talk to your children about how best they can protect their online privacy and ensure they are not open to cyberbullying. Warn your children that if they share suggestive photos or private information via phone or online, even with someone they trust, this can be passed on and quickly distributed more widely. Putting information about themselves online can provide fodder for cyberbullying. Therefore you need to ensure your child understands and uses the privacy settings on Facebook and other social networking sites so that only people they trust can see their accounts, that they only 'friend' people they actually know and are friends with on Facebook and other social networking sites, and that they do not share personal information such as their home address or phone number online.

I believe that parents need to closely monitor the activity of their children on smartphones, computers, tablets, Facebook, Twitter and other devices and sites until they complete the junior cycle in secondary school. You should insist on having the passwords to your child's social networking and email accounts, to enable you to access the messages sent and received. This monitoring should be done in the presence of your child, not in an underhand manner, except when you are satisfied that something very sinister is going on. This monitoring will help you to get a good insight into what is happening in your child's life and it will also inform you if your child is involved in bullying or is the recipient of bullying behaviour or other inappropriate information. I know full well that this advice will prove difficult to implement and many teenagers will refuse to cooperate but at the end of the day it is our responsibility, as parents, to safeguard our children's well-being. I also want to stress that children still at primary school are often involved in cyberbullying or are the victims of it and parents should be proactive in monitoring children from the first time they are supplied with this type of technology.

Bullying and Silence

Bullying can take place in schools and colleges but do not believe that it is in any way confined to such places. Indeed, it is easier to manage in many ways if it is directly linked to a school or college because all schools have (or should have) a clear bullying policy, including strategies to deal with such behaviour. Quite often, however, bullying occurs outside the school and this can be much more difficult to deal with.

The one environment that allows bullying to continue is silence – it acts like oxygen and allows bullies to continue with their campaign of abuse. The reality is that it is not very popular amongst young people to report their peers and there is a huge stigma attached to reporting young people to any authority figure. This is a culture that must be tackled and eliminated. Young people must be free to report wrong-doing in every instance because if not the wrong-doing will continue unabated. The label usually given to those who report wrong-doing, including bullying, is a 'grass' or a 'rat'. It is easy to understand why a young person would not like to get such a label and, as a result, bullying is often not reported, in particular in the early stages, and so it continues. This results in a situation where very often victims of bullying do not report it or even talk about it to others; they just suffer on. You should encourage your children from a young age to talk to an adult about any difficulties they are having in their lives, including being the victims of bullying.

Believe it or not, another reason why victims decide not to report an act of bullying is because they blame themselves – "It's my own fault" or "I must have done something to annoy her." Or, worse still, they make excuses for the bully – "Ah he's not always like that." So the victim is actually feeling self-guilt and staying quiet in the hope that if they themselves change their behaviour the bullying will cease. Again, you should be aware of this possibility and regularly talk with your children about bullying and emphasise that if they are being bullied it is not their fault and that they should never feel sorry for the bully.

A final reason why young people don't report bullying is that they believe that if they do report it their situation will only get much worse, so they remain silent and the bullying continues. Over the past ten years or so much good work has been done by many individuals, groups, schools, teachers and parents to break the silence but the problem continues and much more needs to be done. I will outline later in this chapter how you, as parents, should respond to bullying, including some of the things you should avoid doing.

Why Do Children Bully?

A question many parents ask is "Why do children get involved in bullying in the first place?" Well bullying is actually a learned behaviour, so no child is born a natural bully. There are many reasons why children get involved in bullying and I want to stress that very young children can be involved in what can reasonably be classified as bullying, indeed, from as young as six or seven years of age. Children as young as four years can pick on other children and give them a hard time but because of their age it is unfair to say that they are bullying; I doubt if they really understand the term or fully appreciate the hurt and damage they are causing, but very small children can make life difficult for others.

Back to why people bully – I am aware of a number of reasons why young people will bully:

• Children may have experienced bullying at home; sometimes they are victims of bullying or they witness adults bullying other adults. A home where there is a lot of aggression of a physical or negative psychological nature will often lead to young people going on to copy such behaviour. They observe what is happening and they become aware of the outcomes, for example the bully getting their own way, other family members being in fear of the bully, the bully enjoying the control they have over others, and the bully being a person of power and influence in the home.

- Some children think bullying is great 'craic' and they enjoy the suffering and pain they inflict on their victims, although it is fair to say they do not always fully understand the hurt felt by the victim.
- Some children enjoy the control they have over others; it gives them a feeling of power and superiority. This is often the case when a child is totally controlled at home and is constantly made to feel useless and powerless. Bullying often gives them feelings of power and some people love having power over others.
- Some children bully to show off to their friends and they simply love the attention they get – the class clown syndrome.
- Some young people bully to get rewards like forcing others to give them money, sweets or drugs, or to do their homework.
- Some children bully because they have very low self-esteem and bullying others helps them to feel better about themselves.
- Jealously continues to be a major cause of bullying. This can be around many issues, for example social background, academic ability, accents, and clothes and style.
- Children often observe their own parents or older siblings bullying others in the home or in the community. Indeed, in competitive sporting activities, coaches are known to encourage young players to 'bully' their opponent out of the game.

One other observation – many children who bully often have very little sense of empathy with the pain and suffering of their victims. They might actually feel and believe that they are 'only messing' but this is of little consolation to the victim. Once a child is made aware that their behaviour is having a damaging effect on another child then they should cease that particular behaviour. This is the line in the sand – it is not what the child who is messing thinks or feels; it is how the victim feels.

Bullying Traits to Watch Out For

What types of people develop bullying traits? I have already outlined some of the reasons why people bully, and naturally some of their personal traits are closely linked to this behaviour. But in addition, other traits to look out for are:

- *Deviousness* – Bullies often plan their bullying acts to a very fine degree: they plan when and where to bully, and they pick safe times and places where the victim is often isolated or alone.
- *Manipulation* – A bully is often a type of Jekyll-and-Hyde character and can be extremely manipulative; they can very kind and friendly to some people but vindictive and hard-hearted to others. The bully is likely to be warm and friendly when superiors are present, but cold and cruel when alone with the victim, or among friends.
- *Desire for control* – Some bullies also tend to be control freaks. This is linked to a desire for power and control. The bully wants to make all the decisions and to decide for others; it is a type of dictatorship. The bully will order a victim to do something that they do not want to do like drink alcohol, take drugs, destroy or damage public property, or steal from shops. If the victim refuses they will be alienated from the group and the bully will make life for the victim very difficult and troublesome.
- *Dominance* – A bully will normally have very loyal friends who regard them as a lovely person and will support them all the way when an allegation of bullying is levelled against them.
- *Lying* – Bullies are usually liars and have no hesitation in denying the truth or telling lies about others, and as a result

it is extremely difficult to tie them down and to get them to admit to their behaviour.

- *Cruelty* – Bullies can often be very cruel people and this side of their make-up can be seen in their treatment of animals.
- *Intelligence* – Bullies are often smart and intelligent people who have a capacity to cover their tracks most of the time.

What Type of Child Is Likely to Be Bullied?

Are some children more likely to be bullied than others? The answer is unfortunately yes. Physical features and characteristics are often the main focus of bullying. The list is endless – extremes often stick out like a very tall or a very small child, a very thin or a very overweight child; the colour of the child's hair – blonde or red in particular may attract negative attention; other physical features like their nose, mouth, teeth, eyes, being knock-kneed; having poor hand–eye coordination; and unusual accents, and speech and communication problems are all factors that have the potential to attract negative attention from other children. I must stress that not every child who has a particular personal or unique physical feature will be bullied, but they are in a high-risk category.

Another group of children at risk of being bullied are those with certain personality traits, for example very shy children, very sensitive children, very insecure children and children who feel embarrassed in what would be generally considered normal situations. Children with such personality traits will often attract negative attention from other children and they are much more vulnerable as a result.

Family and social backgrounds can also directly cause negative attention for some children and this too often leads to bullying. This works both ways – children from very socially deprived backgrounds can be at risk of bullying by children from affluent areas, while children from affluent areas can be at risk of bullying by children from socially disadvantaged areas. However, bullying exists within all social status groups.

Major or significant changes in a child's family circumstances can also place a child at high risk of being bullied, such as a parent being charged with a criminal offence; a parent sentenced to imprisonment; a family having serious financial problems; the particular lifestyle of a family – very rich, very poor or being unorthodox or different; parents separating or getting divorced; parents entering into new relationships; or a family taking an active but unpopular public stance on a local political or community issue. Again, I must emphasise that the above mentioned issues don't automatically lead to children being bullied but they often place some children at risk.

Really, *anything* that is different from the normal places the child at risk of bullying – coming from a rural area and transferring to an urban setting or vice versa, having a parent of a different nationality, participating in an activity that would not be normally associated with a particular age or gender, and so on.

Finally, the culture and atmosphere in the school or college that the child is attending will have a big bearing on whether or not the child is likely to be bullied. Much depends on the policy and approach of the school authorities in relation to bullying. All schools are required by the Department of Education to have an up-to-date anti-bullying policy and clear strategies in place, and teachers are expected to take an active role in stamping out bullying if and when it occurs.

So it is obvious that many issues completely outside the child's control can have a major influence on whether or not they will become a target for bullying. However, in a nutshell the more sensitive, shy and different from the norm children are, the more likely they are to be the target of bullying.

Signs that Your Child Is Being Bullied

What should you look out for that might indicate your child is being bullied? A number of factors will indicate that something is wrong but you should not jump to conclusions without having solid evidence and without talking to your child about the issue.

- *Change in behaviour patterns* – Any change in the behaviour pattern of your child should be considered. For example, if they loved going to school but suddenly show a lack of interest and are reluctant to talk about school, or if friends who were regular visitors to your home suddenly stop visiting. A child could begin to express anxiety about going to school or ask their parents to accompany them; for instance, they do not want to travel on the school bus or want to be collected after school. Or perhaps the child's homework is not being done to the usual standard and their school performance has dropped off.
- *Personal items being damaged or lost* – Bullies will often damage or take a victim's school uniform, school books or other personal items. One common example of this is if a child wears a new overcoat to school and returns that evening with it soiled or torn. Often the bully will throw the coat on the floor of the cloakroom as the students are leaving and they will trample all over it.
- *Mood changes* – This is another good indicator but, of course, by itself it is not evidence of bullying. As you will be well aware, many teenagers have mood changes and this is normal, but sometimes it can be an indicator that something is not right. Pay special attention to any positive mood changes that occur on Friday evenings when school ends, following by depression or feeling down in

the dumps on Sunday evenings or Monday mornings when your child returns to school.

- *Dropping out of after-school activities* – If your child drops out of after-school activities for no apparent or good reason this is a strong indicator that something is wrong and you should discuss this with them.
- *Physical symptoms* – Anxiety can manifest itself in physical symptoms, so if your child complains of headaches or a sick stomach, or is not eating or sleeping as usual, this is another strong indicator of potential problems.
- *Constantly looking for money* – Bullies often demand victims give them money or buy items for them, so this can lead to a child constantly looking for more and more pocket money.
- *Physical scars* – If you notice any physical marks or scars on your child this is another strong indicator of potential bullying and should be queried.
- *Nightmares and bed-wetting* – With young children you should be alert to possible bullying if your child is waking up at night after having nightmares or if bed-wetting occurs.

Proving a Case of Bullying

Why is bullying so hard to prove? I have little hesitation in saying that bullying is one of the most difficult of all behaviours to prove and I know of many cases where it actually proved to be impossible to gather sufficient evidence to establish that bullying did occur. There are many reasons for this situation. Firstly, much depends on what form the bullying behaviour consists of – ignoring an individual when he or she joins a group in the school yard is very difficult to prove as a case of bullying. Similarly, if it is a case of one person's word against another's, or trying to trace who started a vicious rumour, this is extremely difficult to prove.

Remember, very few cases of bullying involve physical scars or marks, which can be easily seen. The more common psychological scars, on the other hand, are very difficult to prove. When bullying is done by a group of people it presents extra challenges for victims, parents, schools and others in authority. Group bullying occurs when more than one person is involved in a bullying act. It is often difficult to identify a ringleader as frequently all members of the group take an equal and active part in the bullying. Examples are numerous – consistently excluding a child from an activity like sport, name calling, personalised slagging, gossiping or the spreading of malicious rumours about the victim, damaging the property of the victim, often in their absence – the list is unlimited. This type on bullying is very challenging for parents to resolve as any intervention on their part will most likely only exacerbate the situation for the victims. For this reason you should never jump in and confront the group unless your child's personal safety is at risk. When group bullying is initiated and driven by an individual within the group it is much more straightforward to deal with. However, regardless of whether it is group or an individual, with or without a ringleader, I would urge you not to jump into action without having a well thought-out plan and never before discussing the issue with the victim – your child (see the discussion below on what to do if you suspect your child is being bullied).

Another big problem in proving a case of bullying is getting independent evidence or witnesses to come forward to support a victim of bullying. It is my experience that very few people, young or old, really want to get involved in a bullying complaint process. People often will not give evidence because they are afraid that they will become unpopular with their friends or that as a result they will themselves become targets for the bully. In other cases, the key witnesses are actually good friends of the bully and their allegiance will be to them and not to the victim. It is also very difficult to get independent evidence such as CCTV or audio recordings to back up a complaint.

There is also the issue of interpretation. Only the victim really knows how bullying feels and the hurt and harm it is causing. The reality is that some people are physically, emotionally and psychologically stronger than others and some people have little or no idea how sensitive or vulnerable other people are to hurtful comments, so one person sees an incident as nothing but a bit of slagging and teasing while another person feels hurt and upset. Indeed, I had personal experience of this as a manager when two people who witnessed an incident viewed it in two completely different ways: one thought it was an accident while the other felt that it was intentional. As well as this, the person observing might not be aware that the behaviour they have just witnessed is ongoing and persistent. Ignorance of what is socially acceptable in behaviour terms can also be a factor, but such ignorance must never be accepted as an excuse for bullying. If a person has never experienced bullying themselves they might be unaware of how damaging bullying is for others. As a result, people interpret bullying behaviour in many different ways and therefore it is very difficult to get independent evidence to confirm that bullying behaviour has taken place.

Without hard evidence it is very hard to prove bullying behaviour. Hard evidence is so important because most bullies are devious and manipulative, will nearly always cover their tracks, will strongly deny their involvement in bullying and will have no difficulty telling lies. For this reason independent evidence or supportive evidence is crucial when confronting the bully.

If your child is being bullied it is essential that you discuss the situation with them and try to agree on a strategy. As parents you need to understand the dangers involved in accusing a person of bullying without reliable and well-grounded evidence. The bully or their parents will very likely ask for the evidence against the accused and unless the allegation stands up the accuser can expect a negative response, perhaps even a solicitor's letter within days demanding the production of the evidence backing up the allegation or demanding that the allegation is withdrawn. Not all parents will react like this but some are likely to be very defensive, as I discuss below. Gathering and recording hard evidence is an essential element in processing a complaint of bullying and the first part of your strategy should be to record the facts of every instance of bullying. Facts are powerful, so recording dates, times, locations, names of those present, a brief outline of what occurred and any other relevant details is very helpful when a formal complaint of bullying is being processed. This is why it is generally not a good tactic to jump in impulsively and confront the bully or their parents when you become aware of a case of bullying. The more facts you have gathered together the stronger your case and the more likely you are to have a positive outcome. Remember, bullying is not a once-off incident; it is always a behaviour that is ongoing and persistent over a period of time. The key point to remember is that you need to be careful and to have hard evidence before acting.

What Should You Do if You Suspect Your Child Is Being Bullied?

If you suspect that your child is being bullied, the first rule is that under no circumstances should you rush off and confront the bully or their family. Such a response is certain to fail and is also likely to create new problems for your child. Your very first response should be to sit down and discuss the situation with your child. It is important that this discussion is more of a chat than an interrogation. Parents can sometimes over-react and take over, actually excluding their child from the process of resolving the issue. My advice, however, is always involve your child in the process from the very beginning. If the whole thing is managed in an inclusive and sensitive manner it will be of immense value to your child's development and confidence.

Again, I want to emphasise the term 'chat' – having a chat is always much easier for your child than subjecting them to a serious discussion or interview. Remember, you should treat your children with respect at all times by involving them in decisions that affect their life. Do not pass negative comments like "I'm not surprised that you are bullied" or "Are you sure you didn't cause it in the first place?" or "Ah, you will have to toughen up." Do not hide or conceal any information you have become aware of. Have a full and open chat about the whole situation and, in particular, listen to your child and observe their reaction.

I must return to a theme running through this book – the vital role of listening. I have stated time and again that if parents are good listeners and if they have developed a good reputation as listeners then the chatting process will come easily and naturally and both the child and the parents will be at ease. However, if such a relationship does not exist and parents never or seldom listen to their children then this particular process will inevitably cause tension and stress for both the parents and the child. In this case, much of the initial time should be spent developing trust and reassuring your child that you, the parents, are concerned and not inter-fering and most certainly are not blaming the child. I know of situations where parents began the discussion by asking their child "Why the hell didn't you tell us?" That is not the way to begin the process of dialogue. The child will only hear the words 'why didn't you' and they will immediately feel guilt. To be blunt, if your child did not confide in you there is a good reason for that and unfortunately sometimes it is more the parents' fault than the child's. Of course I understand that often teenagers do not confide in their parents. Some of this is down to teenage culture and the belief that parents do not understand. However, I am convinced that another major factor is the way in which parents react and how judgemental they can be on occasion. This often creates barriers and will block easy communication between parents and their children.

Allow your child time and space to decide how much they are going to share with you. Do not expect everything to be dealt with in one session; indeed, much if not all of the first discussion might be spent building up trust and reassuring your child that it is safe to confide in you. Regardless of whether you are a one- or a two-parent family it is often best if one parent deals with the bullying issue; normally it is much easier to talk to one person rather than two.

During your chat it is important that you have a good understanding of what you want the outcome of your involvement to be and the best way to measure this is to have clear objectives. Sometimes parents want revenge against the bully and forget about their own child and their well-being and feelings. I have no hesitation in saying that your number one objective must be the welfare of your child and the very first step in this process is to ensure that by your actions you do not end up causing more distress for your child by acting impulsively. Some parents do this by, for example, rushing to the home of the accused bully and confronting them or their parents, or by barging into the school and publicly confronting the school principal or a teacher. This will just result in your child being labelled a 'rat' or a 'grass' and they will become even more isolated within their own peer group. Above all, you should never take the law into your own hands and deal with the bully in an aggressive or physical manner.

The first objective should be to not make things worse for the child. The second objective should be to stop the bullying. Any further objectives are a matter for the parents and their child to decide upon. I do not believe in looking for a pound of flesh or making the bully suffer or, for that matter, seeking financial compensation. At the end of the day what to do next is a matter for the individual families involved, but I believe that if you achieve the two main objectives listed above it will be a wonderful outcome for both your child and you. You should decide on what actions to take with the involvement and consent of your child, if at all possible. I am very aware that on some occasions some conflict will arise as a result, for instance, if your child disagrees with all or part of your strategy. Such disagreements need to be discussed and preferably agreement reached with your child. However, there may be occasions when agreement will not be forthcoming and in such circumstances you will have to make a judgement call, always based on what is in the best interests of your child. But, at the very least, ensure that your child's views and feelings are taken on board at every stage of the process.

The one thing that is not an option is to ignore the issue; the hard reality is that bullying is very unlikely to go away of its own accord unless the bully moves from the area or school or is confronted as a result of someone complaining.

After the first chat you should have a good insight into the situation and this should guide you on how to proceed. One of the most important outcomes of the initial chat is to determine if it is, in fact, a case of bullying. If many of the key elements that constitute bullying as discussed above are present, i.e. confirmation that your child is the recipient of ongoing physical, psychological or verbal attacks or intimidation, exclusion or alienation, then your conclusion should be that your child is being bullied. The next important requirement is to establish the facts surrounding the bullying. This is a vital part of the process as facts are powerful supports when the time comes to lodge an official complaint or when confronting the bully. So what sort of facts do you need to know? You should ask:

- How long has the bullying being going on?
- When did it start?
- Who is involved?
- What exactly is occurring?
- Where does it take place?

Knowing the dates, times and locations of incidents of bullying is also important. A major problem associated with many bullying allegations is the lack of hard facts. Many allegations just contain generalisations such as "It happens all the time", "Everyone is involved", "I'm bullied most days", "Some days I'm bullied and some days I'm not", "I can't remember" and "I don't know." The problem is that with the best will in the world it is difficult to prove a case of bullying, so a complainant has little chance of success if facts are absent. Documenting the facts is essential and before any action is taken you must equip yourselves with the hard evidence to support an allegation of bullying.

Ask your child when, where, what, how and who – the answers will provide a strong basis for supporting a bullying allegation. It is for this reason that I always strongly encourage anyone who feels that they are being bullied to accurately record a few facts immediately after each and every incident of bullying. You or your child should note in a diary the date, time and location, what exactly happened, who was present and any other relevant information, and ensure that the diary is kept in a safe place. This will prove to be invaluable in the long term. When the time comes to confront the bully or to lodge an official complaint there will be a strong difference between an allegation backed up with dates, times and precise details of each incident and an allegation based on generalisations. I also strongly urge victims and parents to stick strictly to the facts at all times and to the truth. The truth is always powerful and stands up to scrutiny.

You and your child also need to prepare for the day the bully is going to be confronted or the day of the investigation. As Roy Keane famously said all those years ago, 'fail to prepare, prepare to fail.' Preparation is always essential in any case of confrontation. This is absolutely important in the case of your child – preparation will give them confidence and help them to be strong, especially if faced with denial and false claims from their bully. A few basic principles need to be noted. Victims of bullying must never feel sorry for the bully or make excuses for them. They must never feel guilty themselves or blame themselves for the bullying. You must reassure your child time and time again that they are innocent and that they do not deserve to be treated in such a manner.

You have a number of options when you become aware of an incident of bullying. If the bullying is directly linked to a school the most appropriate response is to make an appointment with the school principal to discuss your child's situation, always in total confidence. Do not confront the school authorities publicly. All schools are required to have a policy and guidelines on bullying and parents should work with the school within the guidelines. Generally speaking, sports clubs, youth clubs and most other organisations involved in youth work have guidelines on bullying and again parents should work with the clubs or organisations when dealing with incidents of bullying. I would suggest that the first and best option is to try to resolve the issue informally if at all possible. If the informal approach fails then make a formal complaint.

If the bullying is not linked to a school, club or organisation, you will have to deal directly with the bully and/or their parents. All persons under the age of eighteen are legally classified as children and you should ensure that the parents or legal guardians of teenagers under eighteen years of age involved in bullying are informed. Never approach an underage bully on your own; if you do you are leaving yourself open to allegations that you have threatened or abused the bully. Child protection guidelines apply in all such cases and you should fully comply with these requirements; it is in your own best interests to do so.

There is an added complication if the bully or bullies are the children of friends or neighbours of your family. Believe it or not, neighbours often react very defensively and negatively when they are informed that one of their children is involved in bullying. This is not put forward as a reason to stop you acting to protect your child, but you do need to be aware that it is likely to occur. It is usually a big shock for parents to hear that their child is involved in bullying and it can take time for it to sink in. However, as the parents of a victim of bullying you have nothing to apologise for and you have an obligation and a right to protect your child. In some cases you may be friendly with the bully and their parents and it might be possible to have a very informal chat about it to try to resolve the situation before taking any formal steps. In some cases this works very effectively and the bullying stops, but you should always be prepared for a less than open and generous response, even from good friends. Remember that most parents will be shocked to learn that their child is accused of bullying and will most likely be defensive. This is a natural reaction and nothing positive will come out of an angry exchange between both sets of parents.

Give the parents of the child accused of bullying time and space to come to terms with their new situation.

If the parents of a child who is accused of bullying refuse to cooperate or respond in an aggressive or abusive manner, then a complaint should be made to the local Gardaí. My advice is that involving either the Gardaí or the legal profession should be a last resort and every reasonable effort should be made to resolve the issues before following that particular road. Irrespective of what course of action you decided to take, formal or informal, the principle of planning your approach, with the involvement and consent of your child, should apply. Gather all the facts together; in other words, be prepared.

Again, I must stress that the number one objective for you as parents is to protect your child and to ensure that the situation doesn't get worse. It is vital, therefore, that your child is fully involved in the process and that their feelings and views are taken into consideration at every stage of the process. For this reason, contact with the school/club authorities or the parents of the bully should be done discretely. Always remember that the second key objective is to put an end to the bullying behaviour. Once this is achieved the whole process has been a success. However, often outcomes are not black and white and ending the bullying is not always easy or straightforward. The one thing that is very important is that you constantly support and encourage your child in coping with the bullying, and when and wherever possible ensure that your child is protected from the bully. Positive feedback and praise for how well your child is coping is helpful. One of the best responses is to help your child to build the confidence to look their bully in the eyes and to tell them that their behaviour is totally unacceptable and that they will not succeed in their efforts to destroy your child's life. This will take courage but psychologically it will do wonders for your child, especially if they are quiet and shy. Of course, your child should never engage in arguments with the bully or get emotional or upset in their presence because this will only show that the bullying is having the intended effect and will likely encourage them to continue with the campaign of bullying. However, the more assertive and confident victims are the better chance they have of coping with the bullying and putting an end to it.

The final essential task is to talk with your child about how unique and special each person is, and how all people are equal and deserving of respect, regardless of physical characteristics or deformities, personality quirks, mental health problems, intelligence, gender, race, sexuality, nationality, wealth, family circumstances or membership of the Traveller community. This is especially important if your child feels like an outsider. You should emphasise the uniqueness of your child and explain how all people are different and that no one is perfect. Reinforcing this, you should *never* make a critical comment or joke about any physical feature or personality quirk of your child or ever tell them that they are thick or stupid or useless. Such comments will devastate your child, make them very self-conscious and totally undermine their confidence. The job of a parent is to boost their child's confidence; incidentally, this should be your role as parents irrespective of whether your child is being bullied or not.

Unfortunately, in some cases of bullying full and final solutions are difficult to achieve for all the reasons discussed above. In my opinion, if you and your child have tried your best and the bullying continues, then choices will have to be made about the future. For example, should a change of school be considered, should the bullying be pursued on a legal basis – which, of course, will be very expensive – or should a move from the area be considered? These are all very serious decisions but if the bullying continues the only other alternative is to continue to support your child as much as possible. Personally, I believe that bullying is far more widespread than many parents understand and many thousands of children and young people experience some form of bullying during their early lives. The best way to tackle and eradicate bullying is by creating an environment in society in general, in schools, in workplaces and in sports clubs in which bullying is rejected by the vast majority of people. Bullying exists mainly because most people who are aware of a case of bullying remain silent and by their silence allow it to continue. When I am speaking to students about bullying I tell them that the real solution is in their own hands. All they have to do is quietly tell the bully to back off; they don't have to report it to the teacher or other authority figure and risk being called a 'grass' or a 'rat'. The silent majority have the power to end bullying. A quiet word to the bully – a clear message by the majority that bullying is totally unacceptable in this school or club – will end bullying. The task for parents, teachers, coaches and students is to foster such an approach, to show that bullying is an affront to decent people and has no place in a modern, civilised and caring community.

What if Your Child Is the Bully?

For any parent, being told that their son or daughter is involved in bullying another child is a big shock. To be honest, it is one of the last things a parent wants to hear. I suspect that most parents would never consider that *their* child was a likely bully and, of course, parents are often the last people to be told or to believe such a reality about their own child. So how should you react when you become aware that your child is accused of bullying? It is very natural to be surprised or even shocked to hear such an allegation about your child but you should always keep an open mind and a non-defensive approach as a starting position. Listen attentively to the complainant and clarify the circumstances and details of the allegation. You do not have to accept that the allegation of bullying against your child is proven at this initial stage but you should undertake to talk to your child about the allegation. Continue to have an open mind and do not jump to conclusions until you hear your child's side of the story. Indeed, my advice is similar to that for parents who have a child being bullied.

The first task is to chat to your child about the whole situation. The age of your child will greatly dictate the thrust of the conversation. If your child is young, say from seven to twelve years old, you will have to lead the conversation and perhaps even help your child to understand what they are being accused of. Again, I must stress that you should not jump to conclusions and accuse your child of wrongdoing until the whole situation is at least discussed. The approach should be done in a calm and relaxed atmosphere. Once the facts are established you will be in a position to decide the next step. Your child might be unaware that what they are doing is actually bullying or they might have some reason for behaving in such a manner. It is vital that you listen to your child's perspective before making any decisions.

If you are satisfied that some element of bullying is occurring then you should explain to your child what is wrong and unacceptable about their behaviour and tell them to stop behaving in this way. It should be dealt with in a calm and orderly fashion and the objective should be to change the objectionable behaviour. It is the *behaviour* that needs attention and so do not make comments about your child as a person, but focus on their behaviour. Once the situation is dealt with it should end there. If this is the first time bullying behaviour is brought to your notice and the first time you speak to your child about it, and provided your child has agreed to stop that particular behaviour, that should be the end of it.

When the child is older, say from thirteen years upwards, the approach should be slightly different. At this stage a child should be much more aware of issues such as bullying and as parents you should recognise this and discuss the subject on a more mature and adult basis. Again, I would strongly urge that the first stage is based on an open chat and your teenager should be allowed to have their say and you, as parents, should listen. If your child believes that they have been found guilty before being given the opportunity to tell their side of the story the whole process will be a failure. There is always the possibility that your child will deny the allegations and even tell lies, but it is much better to allow them to have their say than to jump to conclusions. If your child continues to deny any involvement in bullying and no agreement can be reached I would suggest that a time-out is called and your child is given space and time to reflect on their situation. Do not try to bully your child into an admission. It is important to remember that this whole process could have long-lasting consequences for the future relationship between you and your child. If your child feels that they have been wronged or badly treated by you or that you jumped to conclusions they will not forget what they will perceive as a gross wrongdoing.

I am a great believer in cooling-off time and having time to reflect. Allowing your child time to consider their situation will be time well spent. Firstly, your child might not realise that what they are involved in is bullying behaviour and they are shocked to be accused of bullying. Forcing them to admit to something that they are not aware of as being wrong in the first place is not the best approach and so allowing your child time to reflect on the allegation is a good strategy. This can be a major learning experience for your child and forcing the pace can be a missed learning opportunity. Secondly, if your child is guilty it is equally important that they have the time to reflect and to consider the best way to respond. Your child could also be afraid to admit responsibility because they believe that the consequences would be very serious, so reassure them that you love them and that you are trying to help them. Giving your child time and space to reflect on the situation and to consider their options is, in my experience, a good approach and usually pays off.

You should have a time frame for this reflection period – a few hours is usually adequate but certainly the issue should be revisited the next day. It is important to create a safe and trusting environment for your child by emphasising that you have an open mind, that irrespective of the situation you are there to help and to resolve the problem, and that your love for your child is unconditional. This is not taking the easy option or being soft on bullying behaviour but two wrongs do not make a right and as a parent you must set an example on how to manage and respond to a difficult and complex problem.

Your main objective is to ensure that the bullying or the objectionable behaviour stops. By 'objectionable behaviour' I mean that the accused child feels that they were only messing with or slagging their victim and genuinely did not realise that it was in fact bullying behaviour. In this situation you should explain to your child that this type of behaviour is unacceptable and to cease it. Do not resort to shouting at your child. This will not solve any problems but is very likely to create new and more serious ones in the long term.

It is always a possibility that your child is falsely accused of bullying. This is another reason why you should keep an open mind about the allegation until the evidence is produced and your child has the opportunity to have their say. Unless your child accepts full responsibility for the bullying allegation, I would advise parents to look for the evidence and not to jump to conclusions. At the end of the day it will often come down to your own personal judgement and I would suggest that your judgement is based on the facts and the evidence. In such a situation, strong well-documented evidence or independent witnesses or CCTV footage is very useful in proving a case of bullying and ensuring it is not a case of one person's word against another.

When it is one word against another it is often impossible to be sure that bullying has occurred. If you doubt the truth of an allegation of bullying or have no hard evidence, then the benefit of the doubt should always go to the accused. In this situation, the best tactic is to say this to both parties – your own child and the complainant and their parents – and to closely monitor the situation for a period of time and also to enlist the help of others like teachers, youth workers, team mentors and perhaps other parents. Again, ongoing relaxed conversation between you and your child will help to get the message across that any behaviour that is hurtful or damaging to another child or to an adult is unacceptable and must stop.

In the aftermath of dealing with an allegation of bullying, irrespective of the outcome, you should discuss the issue of bullying with your child and hopefully discover what problems your child has, if any, that led to the allegation. Ask them questions like, "Why did you decide to bully the other child?", "How do you feel now about the victim?" and "How did you feel when you were participating in bullying?" You should also talk with your child about behaviour in general and how important it is to treat all people with respect. It is very important that your child learns from the bullying incident and realises the damage caused to the victim. This is a good time to emphasise that you should be aware that not all bullying by children or young people is exclusively directed at other children or young people. Many children bully adults, like teachers or neighbours, and when speaking to your child you should make it very clear that the bullying of any person, irrespective of age or social status, is totally unacceptable.

It must be remembered that bullying is a learned behaviour and as such can be changed. It is also worth mentioning that children learn much of their behaviour from observing that of their parents. If you are involved in bullying behaviour yourself it will be no big surprise if your child copies that behaviour. Parental example is one of the most powerful influences in your child's development and as parents we must be ever-conscious of this huge responsibility and strive to give a good and positive example at all times and on all occasions. Helping your child to develop and acquire the various personal skills and abilities to enable them to relate to others in a respectful way is part of any solution to bullying. Alongside this, promoting a fundamental respect for other human beings is a very special responsibility of parents and the best way that you can do this is by example – showing respect in all your dealings with other people, in the family home, in the community, in business and in sport and social activities.

Conclusion

Finally, parents, teachers or other adults should never respond to incidents of bullying by telling the victims to toughen up or to just get on with it, or say something like "Ah, it's all part of growing up." It is not any such thing. Bullying is a completely unacceptable behaviour and every person has the right to be who and what they are and nobody should feel they have a right to make life miserable for any other human being. As a society we are far too tolerant of such behaviour. I believe bullying must be tackled head-on and every institution and agency of the state must be proactive in eradicating this social scourge. While this book focuses on parenting and children, I am very conscious that many parents also experience bullying on an everyday basis, in their own homes, in their places of work and in their communities. The one certainty is that bullying will not go away of its own accord. It requires a national educational and awareness campaign to inspire people to root it out of our society. This can be done, provided the majority of people, young and old, refuse to tolerate it. It requires the silent majority to get their voices back and to shout "Stop!"

6

Underage Drinking

Underage Drinking in Ireland Today

In Ireland it is illegal to sell alcohol to persons under eighteen years of age and it is illegal to purchase alcohol on behalf of persons under eighteen. It is also illegal for persons under eighteen to consume alcohol in a public place, but it is not illegal for under-eighteens to consume alcohol, and that is a very significant difference. This situation often causes confusion and anxiety for parents as they are unsure of what approach to take when the question of alcohol consumption is raised by their teenage children. For example, should they allow their teenage children drink wine with meals or should they adopt a very strict stance and not allow their teenage children to drink alcohol at home?

Parents often ask me questions like, "What is the current reality in relation to underage drinking?", "Where do teenagers get alcohol?", "What age should teenagers be allowed drink alcohol?" and "What should I do when I become aware that my teenager is drinking alcohol?" The current situation is that underage drinking is widespread in Ireland and I believe that it is reasonable to say that most teenagers will drink alcohol before reaching the age of eighteen. It is very difficult, if not impossible, to get an accurate figure on underage drinking simply because it is difficult to measure something that is, in reality, an undercover activity. What might surprise many parents is that some children as young as twelve or thirteen drink alcohol on a regular basis, at least once per week, and I have seen children as young as twelve drunk and unable to stand or walk. Parents, therefore, have every reason to feel concerned or, indeed, alarmed. Another big factor for most parents is that they are seldom aware of their children's drinking habits. It is a concealed behaviour and teenagers go to great lengths to cover their tracks.

I believe that children are starting to drink alcohol at a younger and younger age from generation to generation, and so, by transition year in secondary school, many teenagers are pretty regular drinkers of alcohol. Over the past twenty or so years underage drinking has developed into a well-established culture and there is huge pressure on teenagers to become part of this scene. In this context it takes a lot of courage and will power for them to say no to alcohol. The dangers of drinking alcohol at such a young age are numerous and parents should be genuinely concerned. An Irish medical research report published in 2012 showed that there was a fourfold increase since 2002 in the number of young women diagnosed with liver disease due to alcohol consumption. A study of 6,000 young people in Ireland published in 2013 by *Psychiatry Professional* showed that 92 per cent of sixth year secondary school students drink alcohol, with one in four being weekly consumers. The research showed that 83 per cent of first year students do not drink; however, this dropped to 68 per cent of second year students. In reality, this means that one in every three thirteen- and fourteen-year-olds is drinking alcohol. Another finding worth noting is that 11 per cent of teenagers who drink alcohol develop symptoms of emotional and behavioural difficulties. I agree with medical experts like Dr Joe Barry, Clinical Professor in Public Health Medicine and Head of the Department of Public Health and Primary Care at Trinity College Dublin, when they strongly recommend that parents should strive to delay the age at which their children start drinking alcohol for as long as possible. The former British Chief Medical Officer, Lord Liam Donaldson, recommended to parents in 2009 that children under 15 years should never be given alcohol.

Effects of Alcohol on Teenagers

Alcohol is a mood-changing drug and for this reason alone it is unsuitable for consumption by teenagers. Because of their youth and immaturity a very small amount of alcohol can have serious consequences, physically and mentally, for young people. They can easily lose their balance and often fall and cause serious injury to themselves. They are likely to get physically sick and again this can have serious consequences unless they are closely supervised. Young people are also very likely to get aggressive under the influence of alcohol and often this leads to rows and fights, which again place teenagers at risk of serious injury or criminal charges. Under the influence of alcohol, a person's judgement is more likely to be flawed as well, leading to poor decision-making. Indeed, under the influence of alcohol potential dangerous situations are not recognised or they are ignored or under-estimated. So, from a safety angle alone the consumption of alcohol by young people places them at high risk of serious injury. Alcohol also lowers a person's inhibitions, so teenagers are more likely to engage in sexual activities or to take drugs when drinking.

There is little need to point out the health risks that arise when children consume alcohol, either on a regular or a more infrequent basis. The first thing for parents to remember is that a teenager's body, in particular their organs, has not fully developed by the age of sixteen, so alcohol can seriously damage their livers and other organs with life-long consequences. I know many parents who feel that a can of beer will do no harm but what they overlook is that the young person is much more likely to be consuming more than one can at a time. Also, alcohol consumption often leads to depression and young people might not relate their depression to their drinking. Finally, of course, there is the real danger that the young person will develop a dependency on alcohol and this will lead to a serious addiction problem.

A popular part of the teenager drinking culture is binge drinking. This normally involves a group of teenagers drinking five or six shorts in quick succession. Inevitably they all get very drunk in a short period of time. This places them at serious risk on a number of fronts. The amount of alcohol they have consumed will put them at high risk of alcohol poisoning and they may need urgent medical treatment. There is a real danger that they will become semi- or indeed fully unconscious and fall, causing serious injury to themselves. There is also a likelihood that they will get violently sick and place themselves at risk of inhaling their own vomit unless they are closely supervised.

Another consequence of alcohol consumption is that the young person can often feel sick from their alcohol consumption and this in turn will affect their school attendance and concentration levels. I know from talking to secondary school teachers that many teenagers arrive in school on Monday mornings still under the influence of alcohol and in no condition to participate in class activities. Many others do not turn up for school at all on Mondays and as a result they fall behind in their studies and fail to achieve their potential.

Alcohol causes, on average, 88 deaths per month in Ireland. This is a staggering figure; approximately 1,000 people are dying every year in this country as a direct result of alcohol consumption. Some die due to alcohol poisoning, others because of liver failure, many road deaths can be attributed to alcohol consumption, and people under the influence of alcohol are often involved in drowning, fire and other fatalities.

What Do Teenagers Drink and Where Do They Get Their Alcohol From?

Teenagers drink anything and everything that they can lay their hands on – gin, vodka, wine and beer are some of the most popular choices. Vodka is very popular because it doesn't smell and teenagers feel that they can consume it without their parents knowing or even being suspicious.

Where do teenagers get their alcohol from? Believe it or not, most teenagers get their alcohol at home, especially during the early stages of their drinking. They find it in the drinks cabinet and secretly take it out of the house to drink in parks or in other quiet and remote places where teenagers assemble. Parents of children even as young as eleven or twelve years of age should make sure that they do not have unsealed bottles of alcohol around the house as teenagers will take some of the alcohol and replace it with water or other substances. Teenagers will also pour alcohol into a soft drinks bottle to give the impression that they are drinking Coke or 7UP, for example. Many teenagers drink a lot of alcohol before going for a night out and many are actually drunk before they get to the disco or other place of recreation.

Of course teenagers do not depend entirely on the home for their alcohol supply. They will get older siblings or friends to purchase it for them. Their friends will get it in their homes and share it. And, depending on the age and physical maturity of the teenager, they may be able to purchase it in a pub or off-licence. Many will equip themselves with false identification in order to do this.

The 'Free Gaff'

Parents should look out for what teenagers often refer to as 'free gaffs'. A free gaff is a home where the parents are away for the night or for a weekend and the teenagers have the house to themselves for at least one night. A group of teenagers will gather in the house and party all night. This situation – where a huge amount of alcohol is consumed and there is no adult supervision – is full of risks for the young people involved. There is a real danger that drugs could be introduced in this context. Because they are under the influence of alcohol, some teenagers will experiment with, say, smoking hash or taking an ecstasy tablet, when in normal circumstances they would never even dream of taking drugs. Another added danger is that the easy availability of bedrooms will encourage teenagers to engage in sexual activities while under the influence of alcohol. Parents should be aware that children as young as twelve or thirteen can be involved in organising free gaffs.

As a general rule I would say that children under the age of seventeen should not be allowed to stay overnight in a house without adult supervision. Why seventeen? The way I see it, age seventeen is getting close to adulthood. Some people leave home at age seventeen to attend college or to go to work. Parenting is a process and the objective for parents must be to gradually facilitate the growth and development of their child to a stage where they are capable of making sound decisions and, most importantly of all, are mature enough to be able to take full personal responsibility for their decisions.

Another good rule of thumb is that parents should insist on personally checking with other parents when their children are planning an overnight stay, to ensure the parents will be there at all times. Not all parents act responsibly or think like you do, so you should always check. I know of a case where the parents went away for a weekend leaving a sixteen-year-old in charge of two younger children and the home with no adult support.

The teenager went out on the Saturday night and got drunk and the younger children were left at home alone.

I would stress that you should do this networking with other parents openly and with the full knowledge of your teenagers, and not in a sneaky or underhand way. Use your own judgements and instincts in all such situations and do not be influenced by what other parents do. Teenagers will often say "All my friends' parents have no problem with it" or "All my friends' parents don't check on their children." My suggested answer to this would be, "Well, fine for them but we are going to check it out just to be sure that everything is above board and that it's safe for you." It is important to talk to your children about all such issues in a calm manner and to explain the reasons behind your decision. You might end up being told that you are the most unreasonable parent on earth or the worst parent ever, but that is a small price to pay for ensuring that your children are safe. You should also be aware, however, that many teenagers will resent this and will do their best to either stop their parents making direct contact with the other parents or they will try to cover up their intentions by claiming that their friend's parents will be there at all times.

One final point – when children know that their parents cannot be fooled easily they will tell their friends that they can't stay over in the free gaff, for example, because their parents will check it out – problem solved before it even happens!

Why Do Teenagers Drink?

Before dealing with how you should approach the whole subject of alcohol with your children I think that it is very important for you, as parents, to take a close look at your own drinking behaviour. If you are drinking yourself on a regular basis and you are under the influence of alcohol in your own home in the presence of your children it is very difficult for you to lecture your children about alcohol abuse or underage drinking. Now I am not saying that parents are totally to blame for their children's underage drinking or should never drink, far from it, but it is a factor and setting an example is very important. It should not be a case of 'Do as I say, not as I do.' I would also strongly urge you not to normalise alcohol within the home. For example, when you are doing the weekly shopping do not include alcohol as an integral item on the shopping list. Children are very observant and when they see alcohol being treated as a normal part of the weekly shopping it is hard for them to distinguish between healthy food and an alcoholic substance. For this reason I believe that alcohol should be purchased separately from normal foodstuffs and household goods. It is a small thing but I believe that it gives a strong message to children. Indeed, I would go further and recommend that in supermarkets and other off-licence outlets alcohol should be stored in a separate area, away from the main store, with independent access. Again, this would clearly indicate to young people that alcohol is a restricted item and not as normal a substance as milk or fruit juice.

However, parents are not the only influences on teenagers and I am afraid many other factors play a significant role. Teenagers generally greatly admire the behaviour of older teens or young people and long to be able to behave like them and to do the things that they are doing. Twelve-year-olds want to act like fourteen-year-olds, fourteen-year-olds want to behave like sixteen-year-olds, and so on. This is definitely one of the biggest challenges for all parents and it is very difficult to get the right balance. In many ways it is a natural thing and part of growing up. But, in the case of alcohol consumption, there is a huge difference between a fourteen-year-old and a sixteen-year-old. Certainly from a physical perspective alone there is a huge gap and the younger child is at much greater risk.

Teenagers want to sample alcohol to experience its benefits as they see it. In many cases alcohol will give the young person a 'feel good' feeling and it will help to give them self-confidence. Teenagers also like to talk about how 'cool' it is to drink and this in turn leads to a lot of boasting to their peers about how much alcohol they have consumed. In many cases it is seen as a badge of honour to be able to drink large amounts of alcohol; indeed, this is not confined to young people as many adults also like to boast about how much they have consumed in a drinking session. Parents also need to be aware of the fact that many teenagers go through a rebel phase and again it is seen as being very 'cool' to be involved in things that parents either forbid or frown upon.

Group influence and peer pressure are major factors in why teenagers drink. I have long believed that group influence is much stronger and more significant than peer pressure. Group influence kicks in when a group of young people are involved in an activity like drinking alcohol and all members of the group are expected to participate. It is part of the culture of the group. It is very difficult for individuals within such a group to say no because if they do they will feel awkward and apart from the group. Naturally they will come under huge pressure to do what the group is doing. If an individual refuses to participate in an activity like drinking alcohol, it is very likely that that individual will have to leave the group, or even be forced out by the group. The group's attitude will often be, "Well, if you're not doing what we do, you are not one of us." This can be a very tough decision for a teenager to make, and not surprisingly many cave in simply to hold on to their friends. Peer pressure is more straightforward insofar as it involves one person trying to force or encourage another person to get involved in an activity like underage drinking. While this will obviously put some pressure on an individual I think it is often more manageable for a young person than a larger group influence.

Another big factor in why teenagers drink relates to the wider societal culture. Almost every family, local community, and social and sporting event in Ireland revolves around alcohol. It is little wonder then that young people aspire to experience this most widely used and popular drug.

How Should You Deal with Your Child's Underage Drinking?

How should you, as parent, deal with the whole issue of alcohol and how should you respond when you are aware that your child is an underage drinker? As I have already stated, underage drinking is a complex issue and there are no simple or easy solutions to it. The first point to remember is not to react in a dogmatic or aggressive manner. Too often when parents become aware that their teenage child is drinking alcohol they react by shouting at them and then forbid them to drink alcohol again. I can assure you that this approach will most likely not work and, in addition to having a problem with your child being an underage drinker, you will soon have serious relationship problems as communication between you and your child will be seriously damaged or will completely break down. When dialogue and communication are broken or seriously damaged the sad reality is that parenting has also failed. Put simply, good parenting cannot take place in the absence of good two-way communication.

The first task, therefore, is to keep the lines of communication open at all times with your children. One of the best ways of ensuring this is to control how you react when you hear disturbing news. Listen to your child carefully and only respond when you are calm and have fully thought through your approach. You will have to bite your tongue and suppress your anger. Keep the bigger picture in your mind at all times; this is, of course, to help and support your child to make the right choices and to agree to stop drinking alcohol until they are older. As I argue throughout this book, the whole process of communication should start from day one and continue throughout childhood, the teenage years and beyond. You should regularly talk with your children about issues like drugs and alcohol as a normal part of parenting and should not wait for a crisis to start the process.

The best approach is dialogue, information, education and open communication between parents and their children. Of course our educational system has a central role to play in helping children to understand and appreciate the dangers of underage drinking, but parents have ultimate responsibility. One of the biggest parental weaknesses is when parents are totally oblivious to what their children are doing. It is a regular occurrence for parents to be the last people to know what their children are up to when they are outside the home. To counteract this danger, it is a good idea to talk openly at all times about alcohol with your children, and to be prepared to listen to their views and opinions, even when you totally disagree with them. Remember that open dialogue is vital for both parents and children.

A good question to ask yourself when you find yourself face-to-face with your child's underage drinking is, "What is the best outcome for my child?" Because really that is the only issue; everything else is secondary. The ideal outcome is that your child stops drinking alcohol until they are an adult. If that is not possible then the second best outcome is that your child talks about the issue with you and that some consensus is agreed. In order to achieve the best outcome, as stated above, dialogue is key. Talk to your child about your concern for their health and well-being, discuss the dangers of alcohol, emphasise that buying alcohol or drinking alcohol in a public place is illegal for teenagers, and warn your teenager that when they are under the influence of alcohol they are very likely to make poor judgement calls and can easily get into arguments and fights.

A major factor here is the age of your child. I personally would distinguish between teenagers aged sixteen and over and those under sixteen. I fully acknowledge that any young person under the age of eighteen is not legally allowed to purchase alcohol or drink alcohol in a public place but the reality is that young people do drink alcohol before they reach eighteen. I believe that a child under sixteen is far too young to be drinking and that the key objective for the parents is to try to get the young person to agree to stop. Parents should do their utmost to convince their young teen-ager that this is a reasonable position for them to take. While I believe that a child over sixteen years of age should also be strongly encouraged not to drink alcohol until the age of eighteen, I am a realist and I know that thousands of young people under the age of eighteen drink alcohol regularly and they do so with the consent or agreement of their parents. Regardless of the age of your child, you must accept that it is almost impossible to enforce your position on alcohol. The reality is that a fifteen- or sixteen-year-old cannot be physically prevented from consuming alcohol if they are fully determined to do so. Because of this, consensus, and not ultimatums, is the most successful approach.

Conclusion

To summarise, I would encourage you to talk to your children openly about the whole subject of alcohol from an early age, in a serious but matter-of-fact way. I believe that such an approach is far more likely to be successful than being autocratic about the issue. I am convinced that most of the barriers that exist between parents and their children are caused by the attitude and approach of the parents rather than the young people. As I argue repeatedly in this book, reaching agreement and consensus is a much better way of dealing with issues such as drugs and alcohol.

Let us be realistic, young people will drink alcohol whether we like it or not but as parents we can make a huge difference and can greatly influence many aspects of under-age drinking. Setting a good example in our own drinking habits is an excellent starting point.

7

Drugs – An Introduction

I have no hesitation in saying that by far the most damaging and destructive development to occur in Ireland during my lifetime has been the scourge of illegal drugs. Illegal drug use is now widespread in Ireland and is no longer confined to just socially disadvantaged urban areas. Indeed, I believe that it is accurate to say that every town and village in Ireland is afflicted by illegal drugs. As well as the health consequences of drug use, when the savage violence that has become so much part and parcel of the drugs world is also taken in account then it is little wonder that most parents are terrified that their son or daughter would ever get involved in this dangerous scene.

One of the biggest fears that parents have once their children reach the early teenage years is that they will be introduced to drugs. Almost every parent knows that what is frequently referred to as 'using' in reality means that the young person is taking illegal drugs and is involved in an illegal and dangerous activity that has the very real potential of ruining the child's life and almost inevitably the whole family's life as well.

I want to stress at this point that the overwhelming evidence is that most children and young people are first introduced to drugs by their friends and not by strangers or drug pushers. This in itself just adds to the problem for parents. As parents you need to be constantly aware that every teenager is at some level of risk in relation to the use of illegal drugs and you should regularly discuss the issue within the family and on an individual basis with your teenage children. Throughout this book I have put huge emphasis on parents listening to their children and this is yet another example where parents who have a good listening relationship built up with their children will have a big advantage. This advantage is two-fold: firstly, the parents and the teenager will be able to openly discuss the whole drug scene, and the dangers and consequences of even experimenting with drugs. It is also likely that if parents openly discuss illegal drugs with their teenagers they get to hear about what is happening regarding drug use in their local area – who's dealing and who's using. This is vital information for parents as it gives them a good insight into the risks that are out there for their children. Secondly, if the teenager is involved in drugs they are much more likely to confide in their parents, and knowing what is going on in your teenager's life is half the battle.

I must stress that all information you get from your children must be treated with the utmost confidentiality and you must not take any action arising directly from this information unless and until you have discussed it with your children. I have a very good reason for saying this: if you run off and use the information you got from your children in family discussions without your children's consent, the result will be that your children will simply stop talking to you, end of story. If you feel that, for instance, you should report something your children told you to the local Gardaí you should explain the reasons why to your children. You must also remember that divulging drugs-related information that you sourced from your children could place yourselves and your children at high risk if the whole thing is not handled with the utmost sensitivity. The last thing you want is to cause serious difficulty for your children, for example having them identified as informers.

In this and the following chapter I am going to deal with the issues around illegal drugs and teenagers. I hope to inform parents and help them get a better understanding of the drugs scene in Ireland. This chapter is concerned with identifying the most popular illegal drugs used or available in Ireland in 2013, while the following chapter will address the issue of what to do if you believe your teenager is involved with drugs.

While I list the most common signs of use of each particular drug below, I must stress that many of the symptoms are very similar and overlap and it would take an expert in the field of addiction and drug use to recognise the particular symptoms associated with a specific drug. However, these general signs and symptoms will alert you to the fact that your child is not acting normally and appears to be under the influence of some drug or substance. You should look out for general symptoms and immediately seek professional help once you are satisfied that your child has consumed drugs or other illegal substances. However, I would stress that you should not jump to conclusions unless you have hard evidence.

Ecstasy

Ecstasy is often referred to as the 'dance drug' or the 'love drug'. It normally comes in tablet form, although it has been found in capsule form. It is synthetically produced and its chemical name is methylenedioxymethamphetamine or MDMA. The effects of ecstasy start about half an hour to an hour after the tablet is taken and can last for up to five hours. Some of the street names of ecstasy are XTC, Barts, Dennis the Menace, red and blacks, and fun tabs.

Ecstasy is the drug most associated with young people, although it is not exclusively used by young people. Ecstasy can be called the 'love drug' due to the feeling of well-being and friendliness towards others that users can experience. In addition, the drug can have a relaxing but energetic effect. It is this feeling of great energy that gives users the ability to dance for long periods. Ecstasy is a stimulant and this, along with using up lots of energy during dancing, can lead to serious dehydration. In Ireland there have been a number of recorded deaths from dehydration associated with ecstasy use.

Ecstasy tablets come in many shapes and sizes and are usually manufactured in back-street laboratories. The biggest danger for each user is that they have no way of knowing for sure what is in each tablet. Even if people get their ecstasy from the same supplier, the quality of the drug can change overnight, leaving the user exposed to a real danger of poisoning. Ecstasy is usually taken orally in tablet form. Ecstasy users are often introduced to heroin as this is often smoked or snorted in order to bring the person down from the ecstasy high at the end of a night out.

The following are some of the most likely signs of ecstasy use: hyperactivity, unusual confidence, jerky movements, being very talkative, grinding of teeth, very large pupils, sweating, thirst, lack of appetite, staring, spit like a cotton ball and insomnia. Some of the symptoms of the after-effects of the drug are: depression, fear, listlessness, apathy, muscle ache, cramps and mood swings. The cost of ecstasy varies but it sells in Ireland for around €10 a tablet.

Cannabis

Cannabis comes from the plant *Cannabis sativa* and in Ireland is usually presented in the form of dried leaf or resin. Marijuana and hashish (dry grass) are obtained from the same plant. Once it was believed that these plants were grown exclusively in tropical climates but in recent years they have been discovered growing in Ireland, often in huge numbers.

Cannabis has a number of different street names: weed, dope, hash and pot.

Cannabis is cultivated by drying out the leaves and flowering tops of the plant. Its appearance ranges in colour from light green or grey to brown, depending on where the plant was originally grown. In Ireland it is usually sold as a dry leafy material, and sometimes also appears as a tea-like product. Hashish, or hash as it's commonly known, is a compressed resin-type material. It ranges in colour from dark brown to black and usually appears as small blocks or slabs. In Ireland, it is normally consumed through smoking with tobacco as part of a joint. It can also be smoked without tobacco or in pipes.

Cannabis is an hallucinogen. When taken in small amounts, it normally induces a feeling of well-being and relaxation. Even with mild dose levels, people can experience cognitive (rational thinking) and motor (reaction time) impairment. Some users report that, having used cannabis before without problems, they suddenly become anxious and even paranoid when consuming the drug. Also, if a person is already anxious or depressed cannabis has the potential to accentuate these feelings.

Parents should look out for some of the following symptoms if they are suspicious that their child is using cannabis or hash: bloodshot eyes, being distracted or introverted, short attention span, loss of memory, having difficulty in following the user's train of thought, burns on clothes, bits of loose tobacco around the house or in your child's bedroom, and butts of cigarettes without the usual filter stains. The after-effects include heavy smoking of cigarettes and loss of memory.

The cost of cannabis varies and is based to some degree on availability. The more that is available the cheaper it is, but generally a small amount, say a quarter of an ounce, will cost around €20. Cannabis is illegal in Ireland and falls under the Misuse of Drugs Acts 1977 and 1984. If convicted of being in possession of cannabis for your own use, a fine of over €1,000 can be imposed by the court. For a third or subsequent conviction, a prison sentence of up to twelve months can apply.

Over the last year or so (2012/2013), I have been reliable informed that some batches of cannabis now contain a synthetic element that causes very strange and totally unpredictable reactions when inhaled. Young people become very aggressive, are often out of their minds, have no connection with reality and cannot recall their actions or behaviour when they come down from the drug. During this period they are liable to commit very serious assaults on others or seriously damage or injure themselves. I would urge you to counsel your children about the dangers of such contaminated cannabis. This is very important as many young people are constantly being told that cannabis is harmless and has no serious short- or long-term consequences.

Cocaine

Cocaine comes from the pulped leaf of the South American coca plant. It appears as a white crystal-like powder. Crack cocaine is a combination of cocaine and other substances to make small rocks of crack and is smoked by using pipes or 'bongs'. Cocaine was normally sniffed, i.e. into the nasal passage. However, this has changed over recent years and nowadays users often inject it. The common street names for cocaine are coke, charlie, blow, snow and speedball.

Cocaine is widely used in Ireland and is usually pretty freely available. In the old days it was regarded as a rich person's drug, mainly due to its very high cost. However, over recent years, cocaine has become much more widely used and nowadays costs the same as heroin and similar drugs. During the Celtic Tiger era in Ireland cocaine became a very popular recreational drug for many young middle-class people and has been directly responsible for a number of deaths. Nowadays heroin and cocaine are often used together; cocaine to give the user a high and heroin to bring the user down again, and the cycle is repeated.

Cocaine is a powerful drug, though short lasting, and stimulates the central nervous system. It gives the user a feeling of confidence and potency – mental, sexual and physical – as well as dulling the appetite and masking fatigue. Some of the problems associated with its use include nerves becoming 'jangled', paranoia and confusion. After very high doses users can undergo a 'toxic psychosis' and some users have reported feelings of bugs crawling under their skin.

The signs to look out for if you think your child is using cocaine are very similar to the signs of ecstasy use: hyperactivity, unusual confidence, being very talkative, staring, insomnia, lack of appetite and sweating. Cocaine users will also often have nose irritations, such as itching and running, due to snorting, and their heartbeat will be very rapid after use. The kick from cocaine only lasts a couple of minutes and actually wears off within a quarter of an hour. A gram of cocaine will cost around €70 to €80 and crack cocaine will cost about €20 for a tiny rock.

Heroin

Heroin comes from the opium poppy *Papaver somniferum*. It is a strong analgesic or painkiller, and in its legal form, diamorphine, it is used in this regard. It is estimated that there are about 20,000 heroin users in Ireland. In the past heroin use was mostly associated with the greater Dublin area but nowadays heroin is available in many towns and cities in Ireland. Heroin is a most addictive drug and once a person becomes addicted the road to recovery is long and extremely difficult. Some of the street names for heroin are gear, smack, score, deal or fix.

Heroin in Ireland usually comes as a lumpy powder that ranges in colour from white to dark brown. It is normally sold in small plastic wraps for around €20 and each 'wrap' contains just enough heroin for one 'fix' or smoke. Heroin can be smoked, snorted or injected. In Ireland it is usually injected or smoked. Smoking involves placing a small amount of the heroin mixture on a piece of tinfoil and then applying heat until the drug begins to turn into a liquid and it starts to smoke. This smoke is then inhaled through a rolled-up paper or cardboard tube. This method of use is called 'chasing the dragon'. The drug can also be snorted in the same way as cocaine, i.e. by snorting through the nostrils. However, in Ireland the most common use is by injection. Injecting heroin can be a very involved process. The drug user prepares a quantity of heroin on a spoon and adds water or, on occasion, citric acid; this helps to make the heroin powder more soluble and helps to break down the impurities. Heat is then applied to make it soluble for injecting. Most users will apply a tourniquet to their arm to help raise a vein for injecting. This process is referred to by users as 'cooking up'.

Heroin is seldom, if ever, pure. Most pushers add various powders to increase the amount and some of the most common mixtures are brick dust, talcum powder, rat poison and, on occasion, strychnine. Because of this, in addition to the high risk of addiction to heroin, there are other serious health risks.

Heroin can induce feelings of nausea and distress for first-time users. However, those who persevere report feelings of well-being and contentment and for short periods after taking the drug they feel totally oblivious to the reality of the world in which they live. The drug allows them to escape and forget about their problems and worries. When heroin is taken regularly the user quickly builds up a tolerance to it and it is not unusual for heroin users to inject themselves five or six times a day to prevent withdrawals. As a result, many users spend up to €200 a day on the drug and naturally this high cost leads many users to resort to crime to feed their habit. As a result, heroin can have disastrous consequences, not just for the users but also for their families and communities.

Another serious health issue related to heroin use is the sharing of needles, or 'spikes' as they are called by users. Users share needles that have been used by a number of different individuals, thereby placing themselves at serious risk of contracting diseases like HIV or hepatitis. Most heroin users show some symptoms of hepatitis. There are a number of other high risks attached to using heroin. One is the real danger of overdosing, i.e. taking too much heroin at once. This danger is augmented if the user has been off the drug for a period, even a short period, and then takes their usual amount. Because their tolerance levels have been reduced during the period of abstention, the body is unable to cope with the sudden shock of the heroin and the user may collapse and die. Another problem is that, because hygiene is often a low priority for users, the tiny wound created by the needle during the injection could get infected. Unless it is cleaned and treated it will get septic and can lead to blood poisoning. Finally, regular injectors eventually destroy the veins in their arms and legs and some users have lost limbs as a result.

Some of the signs to look out for are very small pupils, very glassy eyes, 'goofing', whereby the user finds it difficult to stay awake or to keep their eyes open, slurred speech, shallow breathing, scratching, loose facial muscles, blood stains on clothes from needle use, bloody tissues, or 'track marks' or needle holes on hands, arms, legs, the groin or the neck. Some of the after-effects are a runny nose or eyes, excessive yawning, agitation, cold sweats, hot flushes and severe diarrhoea. Other evidence of use include burnt tinfoil left around the house or in waste disposal bins, spoons going missing from the home or spoons returned black from heating the heroin, laces or ties in pockets (used as tourniquets), and insistence on wearing tops with long sleeves in warm weather to hide the track marks.

The most up-to-date information I have is that intravenous use of heroin (injecting) is on the decline in Dublin but unfortunately this method is becoming more and more prevalent in many towns around Ireland. The main reason for the decline in Dublin is attributed to the success of the health educational programmes actively promoted by all the drug treatment centres. Although many people still inject in Dublin, more and more heroin users are smoking or inhaling it instead. From a health perspective this is a very welcome development as it greatly reduces the risk of contracting infectious diseases like hepatitis. The big challenge for those delivering health education programmes throughout the country is to connect with heroin users and to get their message across to them.

Amphetamine

Amphetamine is a central nervous system stimulant that boosts energy levels. It can give users short-term good feelings about themselves and also boosts their self-confidence. Amphetamine is an artificially produced chemical that falls under three main headings and brand names: benzedrine, dexedrine and methedrine. The street names in Ireland are speed, whizz, meth and ice.

In Ireland the drug is usually sold in tablet form and is white in colour. However, it is also available as a powder which is white or pinkish in colour. An added problem with amphetamine sold on the street is that it is not pure; indeed, it is often no more than 5–10 per cent pure with many different powders, such as flour or talcum powder, added.

The most popular method of taking the drug is to swallow it in tablet form. However, it can also be snorted in the same manner as cocaine. Amphetamine can be smoked and resembles the 'crack' form of cocaine when used this way. If smoked it is through a pipe or homemade 'bong'. Amphetamine can also be injected like heroin and this is an added concern. Finally, another big concern is that amphetamine can increase libido (the user's sex drive), which may mean that the user will be sexually active with a number of different partners. There is some evidence from other countries to suggest that amphetamine injectors, along with heroin and other drug injectors, can both pose a risk to others and place themselves at risk of getting STIs if they do not engage in safer sex practices.

Because it is a central nervous system stimulant, the drug causes arousal and a greater responsiveness to the user's surroundings. When taken orally in tablet form, the effects usually manifest themselves within fifteen to twenty minutes. These include a feeling of increased confidence and elation, and having a lot of energy. Users can also experience teeth grinding and jaw clenching. In Ireland, amphetamine sulphate is often very popular with injecting drug users. When injected as a powder the effects are almost instant. However one of the big consequences of using this drug is the body 'rebounding' as the drug wears off. This usually happens four or five hours after taking the drug and leaves the user with feelings of exhaustion and often depression. It is also worth noting that some users of the drug will experience 'amphetamine psychosis', which can be very unpleasant.

Parents should look out for unusual and abnormal behaviour or appearances like drowsiness, fatigue, listlessness, blurred speech, looking pale, getting sick, sweating and showing little or no interest in what is going on.

LSD

LSD, more properly called lysergic acid diethylamide, is a chemical derived from the fungus ergot, which grows on rye and other grasses. It is a very strong hallucinogenic drug that has the capacity to alter the user's perceptions. Because of its potency only a very small amount is required to give the user a 'trip'. The street names of LSD are acid, gorbys, micros, shamrocks and Big D.

In Ireland LSD is normally supplied impregnated into sheets of paper or blotting paper. The LSD paper comes in a variety of designs ranging from cartoon characters and flowers to star signs and a host of other designs. Users then swallow or chew the drug-infused paper. This is often referred to by users as 'dropping' acid. The amounts involved can be tiny with each 'micro dot' of the drug measuring no more than 5 mm square. One of the dangers in taking the drug this way is that the user cannot be sure of the amount of LSD that is on each 'micro dot'; this can vary from 50 micrograms, the standard dose taken in Ireland, to 400 micrograms. Most drugs are measured in milligrams (thousandths of a gram) but because of its potency LSD is measured in micrograms (millionths of a gram).

LSD, while regarded as a feelings- and sensations-enhancing drug, can also cause very frightening 'trips' for drug users. First sensations are often excitement mixed with distorted views of the user's surroundings. Effects usually start about half an hour to an hour after taking the drug but can take longer. The effects of the drug will be greatly influenced by the person's state of mind, so if the user is feeling down taking LSD can bring on a 'bad trip'. This can be a dangerous situation in which users may feel the need to harm themselves. Flashbacks can also be a problem for regular users. Some of the signs of LSD use include being either on a high or in a low mood. What will be obvious is that your child is not behaving as normal and will look under the weather.

Sedatives and Tranquillisers

Sedatives and tranquillisers are widely used in Ireland and many adults take some form of tranquillisers on a regular basis. They are taken for many reasons and to treat a number of problems, for example anxiety and insomnia, and in the aftermath of personal trauma. Although these drugs are prescribed, many people can become very dependent on them. In Ireland a huge number of sedatives and tranquillisers are used illicitly by drug users; indeed, they are far more widely used than people believe. Sedatives and tranquillisers have many different brand names and come in many shapes and sizes, but are mostly available in tablet or capsule form. Some of the well-known brand names are Temazepam, Valium, Librium, Rohypnol, Dalmane, Mogadon and DF 118. Some of the street names include ropies, downers and valleys.

Most sedatives are taken orally; however, many heroin users open the capsules and inject the contents. They often crush the tablets and dissolve the powder by heating and then injecting. Parents should note that taking these drugs in this manner is very dangerous as the compounds in tablets and capsules can congeal in the user's veins and cause huge damage.

Sedatives and tranquillisers are depressant drugs that slow down the mind and body. It is dangerous to drive a car or other vehicles after taking these drugs. Heroin users often use sedatives to up the 'high' or they use them instead of heroin. Some of the symptoms that parents should look out for include a sudden change in mood, signs of drowsiness, lack of interest in normal day-to-day life, a change in eating habits, signs of depression and low energy levels.

Solvents

Solvent abuse in Ireland has a long history dating back to the 1970s. The most popular types of solvents abused are various types of glues, but many other household products are also sniffed, such as aerosol sprays, thinners, correction fluids, petrol, gas, paints, nail varnish removers and dry cleaning fluids. Users will often use aerosols that have butane as the propellant. Street names include sniffing, popping, rush and lulu.

When glue is sniffed users will pour a quantity of the substance into a plastic bag and then inhale the vapours. A much more dangerous method is to put a plastic bag over the head to increase the effect. Some substances are poured or squirted onto a cloth and then the fumes inhaled. Aerosols and gas are often squirted directly into the mouth and this can be fatal.

Solvents that are inhaled rapidly have an effect on the brain that is similar to being drunk. Users also experience hallucinogenic effects. There are a number of other effects such as disorientation, loss of control and unconsciousness. The effects on users usually last no longer than half an hour, but of course this can be extended if the sniffing is prolonged. The symptoms, again, are very consistent with those other types of drug use: moodiness, lack of interest in normal day-to-day activities, being sleepy looking and not tuned in to current reality, strange and unpredictable behaviour, and a change in eating habits.

Magic Mushrooms

Psychedelic or 'magic' mushrooms are still used by some drug users and they can be found during autumn growing wild in many areas of the country. The most common type of psychedelic mushroom found in Ireland is called liberty cap because it has a long stem and a unique bell-shaped top.

It is light brown in colour and when dried out has a tobacco-like appearance.

Magic mushrooms can be consumed in a number of different ways, for example they can be boiled and eaten as a soup, they can be cooked and strained and used as a tea, or they can be dried out and eaten. A regular user can consume up to thirty mushrooms at a time.

It is not illegal to eat these mushrooms but it is illegal to process them; in other words, it is illegal to pick them and store them so that they dry out. The chemical found in magic mushrooms is a type of hallucinogen much like LSD. When consumed, magic mushrooms provide an effect that is somewhat milder than that achieved with LSD, but, like with many other drugs, if the user is already feeling depressed or anxious, taking magic mushrooms can often exacerbate their condition. The effects of taking magic mushrooms include hallucinations and nausea. Another danger in using magic mushrooms is that young people could very easily pick poisonous mushrooms by mistake.

Some of the symptoms to look out for are unusual or unpredictable behaviour, a lack of interest in normal activities, spending a lot of time alone, incoherent language or conversation, and looking pale and withdrawn.

Drugs Terminology

The following is a list of some of the most commonly used jargon associated with the drug culture in Ireland, which might be useful for parents to know:

- *Bag* is a small packet of heroin.
- *Bang up* is to inject drugs.
- *Buzz* is the kick people get after taking drugs.
- *Charlie* is cocaine.
- *Chasing the dragon* is smoking heroin.

- *Cold turkey* is when a person is sick after using heroin and is going through withdrawal.
- *Coming down* is when the effect of drugs is wearing off.
- *Crack* is crystallised cocaine.
- *Dealer* is a supplier of drugs.
- *Dope* is a drug.
- *E* is ecstasy.
- *Fix* is an injection of drugs, usually heroin.
- *G* is a gram of drugs.
- *Gear* is usually heroin.
- *Goofing* is nodding off after using heroin.
- *Gun* is a syringe.
- *H* is heroin.
- *Habit* is an addiction.
- *Hash* is cannabis.
- *Hep* is hepatitis.
- *Hit* in an injection.
- *Hooked* is to be addicted or strung out.
- *Joint* is a hand-rolled cannabis cigarette.
- *Junk* is heroin.
- *Junkie* is a heroin user.
- *Mainlining* is injecting into the veins.
- *Naps* are morphine sulphate tablets.
- *OD* is to overdose on drugs.
- *Pack* is a small packet of heroin.
- *Phy* is physeptone, the trade name for methadone.
- *Pusher* is a person who deals in drugs.
- *Roach* is a rolled-up piece of cardboard used as filter in a cannabis cigarette.
- *Shoot up* is to inject heroin.
- *Smack* is heroin.
- *Spike* is the needle of a syringe.
- *Stoned* is to be heavily under the influence of drugs.
- *Strung out* to be heavily under the influence of drugs.
- *Tracks* are needle marks on the skin as a result of injecting.
- *Works* are the needle and syringe used to inject.

8

Your Child and Drugs

Why do young people take drugs in the first place? In my experience, there are many reasons. Young people are inclined to experiment and to try out things that their parents and society in general oppose. Many young people have what could be called a rebellious streak and taking drugs fits snugly with this aspect of their life. Young people who take drugs often tell their friends about the great buzz they get from using. Peer pressure is often a driving force and puts young people under pressure to use. As discussed in Chapter 6 on underage drinking, I believe that group influence and peer pressure are powerful influencers. When a group of young people are regular drug users, the choice is often to use and remain part of the group or refuse to get involved in drugs and leave the group. For many young people this is a very difficult choice. An impressionable young person can also be influenced by older role models who take drugs, including celebrities. Young people love the craic and the buzz they get when they use drugs, and may use simply because of that. Others may be struggling and use drugs to remove themselves from the reality of their painful lives. Young people who lack self-confidence use drugs to give them courage and self-belief. Some use drugs initially during a time of crisis in their lives and then continue after the crisis is over because they enjoy them or because they have become dependent on them. Finally, we must remember that a young person can start taking drugs simply because someone offered them an ecstasy tablet, for example, when they were out one night and they took it because they were caught up in the buzz of the evening, their friends were doing it, and they just wanted to dance and have a good time.

What Is Addiction?

Most parents have a good understanding of addiction. In this case, it means the regular and consistent use of drugs even when the person knows that they are causing real problems for their health and well-being. After a period of drug-taking a person develops a serious dependency. When addiction and dependency are combined the drug user develops serious problems, problems that are seldom confined to the individual but gradually filter outwards, bringing in family members and often the local community.

The central problem is often that the addiction and dependency are stronger and more overpowering than the user's own will power. Our will power generally keeps us all on the straight and narrow. Sometimes we get the urge to do something that is exciting but wrong or illegal; however our will power ensures that we resist this impulse. This applies across every element of our lives. If we break the speed limit while driving we slow down because we are afraid we will get caught or because we believe that we are putting ourselves and other road users in danger. When we are hungry and have no money and we see food openly available in a shop, our will power tells us not to rob. Our will power is normally a very effective control device. However, once a person is addicted to and dependent on a substance, the power and influence of that dependency becomes much stronger than their will power. Even if they realise that the drug is causing them serious damage, they ignore their inner voice, their will power, and continue on regardless. This is the stage at which the addiction and dependency completely control the person's life. This control has much broader ramifications than just the drug use; it also controls all of the person's behaviour and actions. It is not surprising, then, that the person starts to rob to get the money to buy the drugs. They stop keeping appointments like turning up for work or college. They start telling lies. They become completely undependable, and awkward and ungrateful at home. In other words, their whole life will become totally dominated by their dependency on drugs.

It is important to know that once a person becomes addicted to a drug, two separate dependencies are usually present, physical and psychological, and this is the main reason why addiction and dependency are so difficult and complicated to break. Physical dependency is when the drug user needs the drug to prevent them feeling sick and to prevent withdrawal symptoms. Psychological dependency occurs when the drug user repeatedly uses the drug to obtain emotional security and to relieve stress and anxiety. A person can start out taking drugs for stimulation and enjoyment reasons and over time become dependent on the substance. So it becomes a psychological 'crutch' for that person, who believes that they cannot cope or live without the drug. This psychological dependency is often far more difficult for the individual to deal with than the physical need for drugs.

So what often starts off as a bit of fun for the young person and nothing more than the normal risk-taking that is part and parcel of teenage years can quickly turn into a nightmare experience. A huge part of the problem is that quite often the young person gets a thrill and feels on a high after taking drugs for the first time, and they want to feel that way again. However, many drug users say that their first experience of drugs was never fully replicated again, no matter how many times they took drugs subsequently.

Drug Tolerance and Withdrawal

A key aspect of drug use to be aware of is drug tolerance. The longer a person uses drugs the more of it they will need to get a kick, as their body builds up a greater and greater tolerance to the drug. One of the dangers of drug use, therefore, is if the user gives up for a period and then resumes the habit and takes the same amount as they were taking previously. During their break from drug use, even over a short period of a few weeks, their tolerance for the drug will have reduced, and so taking their 'normal' fix at this time will put them at risk of an overdose or adverse reaction. Another complication can arise when the quality or strength of the drug increases. For example, the heroin sold on the streets is typically scaled down in terms of its purity, to perhaps as low as 20 per cent in some instances. So if a user is given a supply that is much purer, say 50 per cent pure, this will automatically greatly increase the risk of overdosing. Unfortunately, the user will have little or no idea of the strength of the fix they are taking.

A term often associated with drug taking is 'withdrawal'. This is the term given to the user's physical reaction to the cessation of or a reduction in drug intake. Drug users avoid this feeling by taking more drugs. However, going through withdrawal without medical and counselling support can be very difficult, horrific for some people. Going through withdrawal without medical help is known in the drug culture as 'cold turkey'. The user gets very sick and feverish in most cases, sweats profusely, vomits, shivers, shakes and raves – it is a really horrible experience. Of course, in addition to the physical pain there are also serious psychological consequences to withdrawal, with feelings of depression, sadness, hopelessness and failure very likely. Parents should keep an eye out for such symptoms if they are suspicious that their child is using drugs.

General Signs and Symptoms of Drug Use

In the previous chapter I outlined some of the signs and symptoms to look out for in relation to specific drug use, but I now want to identify some general signs. Firstly, keep an eye out for the presence of any of the following items or signs:

- Roll-your-own cigarette papers with filters – these could be for ordinary cigarettes, known as roll-ups, but if the child doesn't smoke normally then they could be a sign of cannabis use
- A burnt aromatic smell, which could indicate cannabis use
- Blackened or burned spoons, which could be used to heat heroin
- Syringes or needles, which are used for injecting drugs
- Plastic bags with glue residue, which could indicate glue sniffing
- A large number of spent matches or used cigarette lighters in a room
- Some drugs like cannabis give off a very strong smell and this can often be picked up on the user's clothes and breath

Also keep an eye out for pills, pill boxes or small bottles. Again this could indicate someone taking drugs. Pills are very widely used by young people and they are just as lethal as any other drug.

Secondly, keep a lookout for some of the following behaviours:

- Secrecy about activities and your child's whereabouts at certain times. Remember that most teenagers will behave strangely around their parents, so secrecy on its own is not proof of drug taking.

- Keeping very late hours is another indicator, as is the sudden arrival of a number of new and strange friends. When the two are combined together, along with secrecy, then you should pay attention.
- Your child's money requirements are another good indicator. Drugs are very expensive and any teenager who is a regular user will spend a significant amount of money each week on their supply. Parents might ask "What is a significant amount?" It really depends on how heavy their use is but it's accurate to say that even a small-time user will spend at least €100 a week on drugs and many users spend hundreds of Euro every week. So, keeping some tabs on the pocket money your teenager is spending is an idea. If they are always short of money and looking for more than their weekly allocation, it would be good to find out why. Again, I must stress that a teenager might be always short of money for other reasons and this on its own is not an indicator of drug use. You should also be alert to money going missing in the home. This should be taken seriously as it is certainly an indicator of some financial pressure on your child.
- Take notice of any mood swings by your teenager or outbursts of temper or violence. Of course, mood swings are part-and-parcel of normal adolescence but, again, a number of indicators coming together are suspicious.
- Drug users often have memory loss and very short attention and concentration spans.
- Changing eating habits are also indicators. For example, if your child was always a good eater of food but suddenly stops eating their meals and is looking gaunt and run down, this should be kept under observation.

The parents of young teenagers who became drug users often told me that, looking back and with the benefit of hindsight, they could see many of the signs and symptoms that I have outlined above, but they never linked them together and never thought that drug use was a possibility for their children. Indeed, I think it is often the case that parents are the last to realise when drug use is occurring.

Monitoring Your Children

As a rule, I do not believe that parents should operate under-cover in their own home, sneaking around trying to catch their teenager out. I would not say that such a tactic should never be used, but it certainly should be regarded as a last resort. If parents have previously expressed their concerns about drug use to their teenager, who has given firm commitments that they are not using or that they have stopped, but these commitments have not been honoured or the teenager's behaviour continues to cause alarm, the parents may feel that they have no alternative but to under-take some form of surveillance to uncover the truth. I know of many parents who discovered drugs using surveillance methods and then aggressively confronted their child, blowing their cover within a few seconds and destroying their relationship with their child. Therefore I must repeat that while this approach can have short-term benefits, it will certainly have serious long-term consequences for the parent–child relationship, which can undermine attempts to get your child into treatment and make it difficult for you to support your child as they battle their addiction.

What to Do if Your Child Is Taking Drugs

So what should you do if you become aware that your teenage child is using drugs? First, I must warn you against over-reacting. This will often do more harm than good in the long term. This is not to suggest that you should go soft on the issue or not take it seriously. Drugs are a very serious matter, not only potentially leading to addiction and dependency but also the possibility of a criminal conviction. If you discover that your child is using drugs you should take the time to discuss and plan your response and perhaps seek professional advice. Do not burst into action and go straight for the jugular; the worst time to confront your child on such a serious matter is when you are upset, stressed and angry. Take the time to think about the most desirable outcome for your child, and act accordingly.

With this in mind, a good starting point is to have an open and totally non-judgemental chat with your child about the whole situation. Throughout this book I have emphasised how important it is for parents to have good open communication with their children from a very early age. It is on that basis that I suggest you should have regular and ongoing discussions about drugs with your children long before their teenage years. If such dialogue is normal then you will find it easier to discuss any concerns you have about drug use with your children. Such a discussion helps you to get a good insight into your child's mind and some indication of how involved they are in the drugs scene. Your child is given the opportunity to build up trust in you and to feel confident that they can share their situation with you. Remember that teenagers generally believe that parents are old-fashioned and out of touch with modern culture and that, as a result, they would be shocked if they knew that their child was using drugs. Now of course any parent would be shocked to hear that their teenager is involved in drugs, but my advice is to control your reaction and not to get aggressive or abusive with your teenager. Hard evidence shows that this seldom works and most certainly does not deal with the personal issues that your child might have. It also does not deal with any addiction and dependency problems.

Your next steps will depend on how seriously your child has become involved in drugs and whether or not a dependency or addiction has developed. If they are just experimenting then your immediate objective is to help your child understand the dangers of drugs and their potential to destroy their future, thus getting their agreement that the drug-taking will stop. If, on the other hand, your child has developed a serious addiction and dependency then the challenge is much more serious and will require the help and advice of drug treatment experts.

The ideal situation is that your child comes to the conclusion that they need help and want to seek it. An absolutely essential requirement is to get your child's agreement and consent to whatever course of action you want to take. When someone has developed an addiction to drugs there is no magic solution. The road to recovery is usually a slow and painful journey for all involved and you should prepare yourselves for many setbacks and disappointments along the way.

However, it is likely that your teenager will have a different view on how serious their level of addiction is. One of the biggest problems when helping people suffering from any type of addiction is the huge level of denial that many people have about their addiction. They simply either do not accept or, worse still, do not realise the presence of addiction. A frequent comment is, "Oh, I use drugs alright but I can give them up anytime I like." Very seldom is this true and while the addicted person holds on to this view it is very difficult to help them. However, it is not impossible. The best way to help a person in denial is to talk the whole situation over with them and share information with them about drugs and how people become addicted. This process may take weeks, so, again, it is important that you don't try to force progress or an admission of addiction. I must also stress that for any person to acknowledge and accept that they have an addiction is a very traumatic experience and it is often the beginning of an extremely difficult journey for the addicted person. This is the reason why the pace must be set by the addicted person rather than others; it often takes people a number of weeks or even longer to reach the point where they feel safe enough to make such an admission. I fully acknowledge also that some people do not actually realise that they are addicted so for such people the process can be very difficult and, indeed, shattering.

Deciding on the appropriate intervention depends on the seriousness of the addiction. Some people will need medical intervention and others residential treatment, while still others will be able to cope with support from family members or professional counselling. It is important to understand that there are many different approaches when responding to people who have addiction problems. For example, some people respond very well to setting goals of abstinence, just adopting a one-day-at-a-time approach. For others who have serious addiction problems, the best options are often a harm reduction approach, for example for heroin users this may mean opting for a methadone course. Methadone is a prescribed drug which acts as a substitute for heroin. At the end of the day much will depend on the individual; some people will be able to tackle their addiction head-on and they have the capacity to cope with the physical and emotional pain. Others are simply unable to cope without some medical and emotional support.

As parents you can provide huge support for your addicted teenager but the skill is not to be too pushy and not to take over the decision-making process. The course of action to take must always be at least a joint decision or, better still, the sole decision of the addicted person. The chances of success are much higher if the treatment decision is taken by the individual who has the problem. If you have an addicted child I would strongly urge you to seek help and information on addiction yourself as soon as possible. Knowing the various stages of recovery and how each stage fits into the whole healing process is vital and will provide great reassurance and support for you, and enable you to better support your child. I must also warn that, even when the addicted person is fully committed to treatment and recovery, there is always a real danger of relapse. Changing behaviour is very difficult for most people and that applies to much more than addiction. Think of the difficulty people have with such simple things as sticking to a diet, taking exercise on a regular basis or ending a bad habit like biting your nails. Many addicted people find it easy enough to stop using drugs; their real struggle is to stop using indefinitely. You also need to accept that your child is an individual, and what works well for one person may not be the solution for another.

If the number one objective is to help your teenager to stop using drugs, then the second objective should be to try to discover why they opted to use drugs in the first place. This is vital information because if the reason for the drug use is not addressed it is very likely that drug use will resume over time. Remember always that the most important outcome of all this is that you can continue to chat with your child.

What about how the young person got the drugs? First, you must understand that providing information about drug dealers is often far more complicated than people might think. One of the main pillars of the drug culture is that those involved in it do not give information to anyone about where they get their drugs or any details about the drug dealers. This is part of the reality of the drugs culture and savage violence is the most common response of drug gangs to any divulgence of information. Therefore, it will often take time before your child provides any such details to you. If they do so, it is your duty as parents to make sure that the information does not get back to the drug dealers. I am not saying that this culture must not be tackled but I do honestly believe that parents on their own should not tackle it and they need to be very aware of the real dangers for their child. One issue that often arises for parents is should they inform the Gardaí. My advice is that you should seek the help and advice of your local Gardaí. The Gardaí are very conscious of the dangers that I have outlined for drug users and they will treat the information provided by you in the strictest of confidence. It is also essential to realise that having illegal drugs stored in your home is a very serious criminal offence. I do not want to scare you unnecessarily, but this is something that you should keep in mind and you should not get involved in any form of cover-up for your teenagers.

Conclusion

One of the big tasks for us as a society is to get a good balance in relation to how we deal with illegal drug use. On the one hand, if we are too soft on the issue it is likely that young people will feel that drugs are not a serious or danger-ous issue. But, on the other hand, if society's attitude is very antagonistic and totally negative, the mythology that surrounds drugs will continue and young people, in partic-ular the rebellious ones, will only be further attracted to them.

The best advice I can give is to repeat that you must never over-react, no matter how serious the situation is, and that you should try, as much as possible, to keep the lines of communication open with your children at all times. You may need to bite your tongue on many occasions and to keep control of your emotions and your temper simply to ensure that this remains the case.

Finally, you should keep yourselves informed about the current drugs scene and keep an eye on whether or not your children are using drugs. You should talk openly about drugs and the dangers they present with your children, and listen to their views on this issue. Be very careful not to jump the gun and accuse your child of drug-taking unless you have reasonable grounds for concern. Constant and ongoing dialogue with your children on the issue of drugs is the best approach, so if the day arrives when you are concerned it will be much easier to discuss the issue in a calm and reasonable manner.

9

Suicide

I have no hesitation in stating that by far the most traumatic experience for any parent is when their child decides to end their life by suicide. I know that the death of a child in any circumstances is a terrible experience for parents, but I believe that the tragedy is augmented if the death is the result of suicide. Unfortunately, the number of young people dying by suicide in Ireland is growing at an alarming rate. Suicide may be something that you, as parents, seldom, if ever, think about. But with the recent tragedies in the news, perhaps it is at the back of your mind. For some parents, however, it is a constant worry, especially for the parents of young people who suffer from depression. Sadly, suicide is touching more and more families around Ireland. A significant number of teenagers have attempted suicide and many have died by suicide. The most recent statistics are for 2011 and they show that 525 people died by suicide in 2011, 439 males and 86 females; the highest risk category is 15- to 24-year-old males. However, it is widely accepted that the real figure for suicide in Ireland is much higher as many deaths by suicide are not reported or classified as such, for example some road deaths, drownings, accidents and drug overdoses. In 2011, 9,824 individuals presented at hospitals following deliberate self-harm. The peak age for women was 15 to 19 years and for men 20 to 24 years.

Why Do Young People Decide to End Their Lives by Suicide?

There is no one common reason for suicide and in many cases it can never be known for certain why the young person made the decision to die. However, the following are some of the most common factors associated with suicide:

- Mental health issues, including acute depression and schizophrenia
- Believing that they are in a hopeless situation
- Physical health problems
- Drugs and alcohol addiction, causing mental illness and serious depression
- Being victims of bullying
- Copycat behaviour (this can happen in the immediate aftermath of the suicide of a close friend or school mate)
- Social alienation
- Family disputes or rows
- Feelings of shame
- Being unable to cope with their situation, for example having serious financial problems
- Believing that an action or a behaviour they are responsible for has brought social disgrace upon themselves and their family
- A broken relationship
- Being caught up in violent feuds
- Owing money for drugs, being unable to pay up and feeling terrified of the consequences
- Feelings of failure and of letting their family down
- Revenge against others, including parents, teachers or personal friends

It is important to say at this point that people who die by suicide or attempt suicide come from every stratum of our society. Parents should fully accept this fact; having all the material support one needs, living in a very affluent area or attending a well-known college – and from the parents' perspective wanting for nothing – is no guarantee against the feelings of hopelessness and despair that can lead to suicide. In fact, a more affluent background can bring its own troubles, including high expectations from parents and teachers that can lead to feelings of failure. All of us are fragile at various stages throughout our lives and social status and material supports have little if any bearing on our psychological well-being.

Myths about Suicide

Before discussing this any further, let me put a number of myths about suicide to bed:

- *If a person talks about suicide they are very unlikely to actually die by suicide* – This is certainly not true; about 80 per cent of people who die by suicide will have spoken about it as an option for them prior to their death. Therefore you should take any talk of suicide by your teenage child very seriously and reassure them that suicide is not a good option and that all problems can be resolved.
- *If a person is determined to die by suicide they will succeed and there is nothing anyone can do about it* – Not true; many people who have been close to completing suicide have, with help and support, come back from the brink and gone on to lead very happy and fulfilling lives.
- *If a person inflicts very minor injuries to their body it is not very serious and is not an indication of serious suicidal intent* – Again, not true. Any person who self-injures is certainly crying out for help and to ignore it is not an option. I know many people who often self-harmed, some to a serious degree, and they are still alive and living normal lives. However I also knew people who initially just scratched

themselves, but subsequently went on to die by suicide. The reality is that it is impossible to know exactly why a person self-harms. Any incident of self-harm by your child should be taken very seriously and you should definitely talk to the child about the issue and seek medical attention.

- *Only people with diagnosed serious psychiatric problems attempt suicide* – Again, this is totally untrue. Of course mental illness is a factor in many suicides but parents should not be fooled into believing that all people who attempt or die by suicide are suffering from a diagnosed mental illness. This also throws up another question: as a society where do we place depression? Depression can range from major or clinical depression, which needs the help of a medical or psychological professional, to milder and more temporary episodes of sadness. Some form of depression strikes most of us at some point in our lives. Depression is a massive factor in many completed suicides; some research shows that up to 90 per cent of people who have died by suicide suffered from depression. The big problem is that many people, young and old, feel low and down at times in their lives but this is not acknowledged by them or their immediate family or friends. In many instances the individual does not recognise that they are suffering from depression and they seek no help or do not mention their low mood to family or friends. Remember that for many people acknowledging that they are suffering from depression is very difficult as there is still an element of stigma attached to it. One of the things that you, as parents, can do to tackle this problem is to talk openly about issues like mental illness and depression with your children in a normal and routine manner. The main message is that if your child has never been diagnosed as suffering from depression or has never raised the issue with you that is not in itself a guarantee that they are not depressed. You should also be aware that a single traumatic incident in a young person's life can cause depression.

- *People who talk about suicide or cause minor injuries to themselves are doing it just to attract attention* – Of course there are a small number of people who do manipulate others and situations just to be the centre of attention, but I can vouch for the fact that many an individual who was regarded as an attention seeker subsequently died by suicide. This was often the direct result of people failing to respond to their cries for help. I would therefore strongly urge you not to ignore the cries of a person who is regarded as an attention seeker.

- *When a person is determined to die by suicide they will not confide in anyone* – Again, this is simply not true and many people are alive and well today as a direct result of a close friend or family member reaching out to them when they were in a crisis; indeed, evidence shows that many people who died by suicide were ambivalent about doing so right up to the time of death. I am convinced that many people who die by suicide do not really want to die but want to get away from their emotional pain or from what they regard as a hopeless situation.

- *It is not good to raise the issue of suicide with people as this might put it into their heads* – While this may be true in a tiny number of cases, I believe that talking openly about suicide with those who are feeling depressed or in a hopeless situation is much more likely to help them, by showing them that you care for them and by encouraging them to seek professional help.

- *Perhaps the person is better off dead* – I do not accept such a negative attitude and strongly believe that the vast number of people who die by suicide do so because they cannot find a solution to their personal problems or emotional pain. Many people who contemplated or attempted suicide in the past now live happy lives because they received help and support at the appropriate time.

What Are the Signs of Suicidal Thought?

It must be remembered that every suicide is an individual case and some young people deliberately mislead everyone about their intentions. So, while the following indicators of suicidal intent are very helpful, this is far from a complete list. I will also remind you that many of the behaviours described below can also be present at various stages in a young person's development and are not, on their own, signals that they are contemplating suicide. With that proviso, these are some of the more common indications that a young person is considering suicide:

- *A significant change in a person's normal behaviour* – For example, a person who is usually an extrovert suddenly becomes introverted. In other words, a young person who was always out and about and involved in all sorts of activities with their peers suddenly starts to stay in their room for hours and hours and seldom, if ever, mixes with other young people. Equally, a person who is a very diligent worker can suddenly become careless, lackadaisical or disinterested in their work or studies. You should discuss this issue with your child in order to ascertain if there is a logical reason for the change in behaviour. Indeed, I think it is fair to say that any major or sudden change in behaviour should be discussed with your child or teenager. I stress that this in itself is not an indication that the young person has any suicidal thoughts, but it could be a sign of bullying, involvement in drugs, depression, or another personal problem.
- *Mentioning thoughts of suicide or self-harm* – Pay close attention if your child discusses such thoughts. If necessary, discuss such incidents with your family doctor, the school chaplain or some other competent person. Do not ignore it. Just because a young person has thoughts about

suicide does not make it inevitable that they will actually attempt suicide, but it is an indication and it should be teased out with them.

- *Mentioning feelings of failure* – Any comments from young people that they are a failure, they have no hope, they are a loser, they would be better off dead, they are nothing but trouble, they feel useless, and so on should alert you that something is not right and that your child is under stress or pressure. Again, talk to them about your concerns.

- *A sudden and serious lack of interest in their personal appearance, including personal hygiene* – This should be discussed with your child, focusing on the reason for the change in behaviour. Some parents confront their teenager about their personal appearance and order them to clean up their act without even mentioning why they have lost interest in their appearance. If this is a change from their usual behaviour query why it is happening, as it can be a sign of inner turmoil. On the other hand, I know that many teenagers often pay little attention to personal hygiene and if this is the norm for them then it is not an indication of any personal problems.

- *A significant negative and sustained change in mood* – Mood swings are normal in puberty and are generally nothing to worry about. However, a significant negative and sustained change in mood can be a clear signal that the young person is under some pressure and you should discuss this concern with them. Once again I would urge you not to make a big deal out of it; this should be a casual and relaxed chat, not an interrogation.

- *Other recent suicides* – Parents should keep a close eye on their child in the immediate aftermath of a close personal friend or school mate dying by suicide. There is a real danger that one suicide can lead to another, as a result of copycat behaviour. If your child makes any favourable comment about a suicide this should be taken very seriously. Comments like, "I wish I had the courage to do it", "He was so brave", "She's a hero" or "I wish I was with him" should always be probed further. Similarly, if your teenager idolises a celebrity who has died by suicide, or constantly plays music associated with death these are other indicators that need discussion.

- *Irresponsible risk-taking* – Taking risks such as driving at high speed, jumping into water from great heights, climbing onto high roofs, or going out to sea without the necessary equipment or ensuring that other people are aware of their whereabouts are all actions that should spark a discussion with your child.

- *Discussing funeral arrangements* – If your child gives any instructions about the type of funeral service they would like in the event of dying suddenly or if they recommend the type of music or songs they would like at their funeral you should discuss with them why they are planning such details.

What Should You Do if You Think Your Child Is Suicidal?

So what should you do if you fear that your child is suicidal? The most important thing you can do is talk to and listen to your child. Tell them that you are worried about them and gently ask them to tell you what is wrong. Reassure them that you will not get angry with them and tell them you will help them resolve their problem. It is here that having a safe and non-judgemental environment in your home is key. Indeed, if such an environment is in place in your home the likelihood is that your child will have discussed the problem with you before it becomes a crisis.

You should seek help if and when you are satisfied that your child has serious suicidal thoughts. In the first instance, this should be done with the consent of your child but if this is not forthcoming then you will have to make a judgement call. If you are genuinely concerned about the suicidal intentions of your child you should seek medical advice. An important question here is does your child suffer from depression? If the answer is yes then your child needs medical attention. However, if your child has never shown signs of depression then you will have to consider the possibility that perhaps they are suffering but undiagnosed. Many young people suffer from depression and modern treatment is very effective in controlling and curing it. Those suffering from serious depression certainly need medical help and your first priority must be to encourage your child to visit the family doctor. You should be aware that many young people feel that to acknowledge or accept that they are suffering from depression is very sensitive and difficult for them and you must treat the whole issue with the utmost privacy and confidentiality.

If you are satisfied that your child has serious suicidal intentions you must keep them under close supervision until medical help has arrived. In reality this means that your child is never left alone for any period of time. However, you cannot continue to provide such supervision indefinitely. Once the initial medical examination has taken place and treatment, if any, is provided, the question of close supervision must be addressed on a more long-term basis. You should be aware that young people who are determined to die by suicide will do their very best to mislead and distract their parents, family and close friends. For example, in the lead-up to a serious suicide attempt they are likely to act as if they are on top of the world, giving the impression that they are enjoying life.

I must stress that only a tiny number of young people who suffer from depression or other mental illnesses are suicidal and the vast number of people who are suffering from depression never consider suicide as an option.

However, depression is a contributory factor in many suicides and, at the very least, parents need to be vigilant when their child is suffering from depression. Nevertheless, suicide is not confined to those who suffer from depression, as many people who die by suicide were never diagnosed with depression.

In many ways it does not really matter why your child is considering suicide; the only thing that really matters is that they get help. This can be a very difficult issue for parents. After talking with your child, or at the very least attempting to do so, you will have to decide what is needed. If your child is not cooperating or agreeing to your suggestions then you will have to decide the next step. Much will depend on the age of your child, for example a child in their early teens is still very much a child and you have ultimate responsibility so you must decide the next step. You should certainly talk to people like your child's teachers, sports coaches or youth club leaders to ascertain how your child appears to them and if they have any concerns. When your child is in their late teens it is often much more difficult to make decisions for them; often they simply will refuse to see the family doctor or a psychologist, psychiatrist or counsellor. There is little you can do if your child refuses to accept your help but keep talking and listening, and eventually they might respond.

Finally, sometimes, despite the very best efforts of parents, young people will die by suicide. On many other occasions children will die by suicide without ever giving the slightest indication that they had such plans. Parents can only do their best and, as I have stated time and time again, one of the best ways of knowing how your child is doing is by having a safe, secure, confidential listening environment in place for your child.

Providing a Safe Listening Environment

As I have emphasised time and time again in this book, the best approach for parents to any problem is to listen to their children as much as they can and to be as tolerant and non-judgemental as possible. Many teenagers feel that they cannot possibly confide in their parents or share their problems with them mainly because of how their parents might react. Teenagers have knowledge, gained from experience, of how their parents will respond in any given situation. Many teenagers have said to me that they would be terrified to talk with their parents about many of their personal problems. Some of the most frequent examples of such problems are alcohol or drug-related issues, problems of a sexual nature, bullying, relationship problems and physical or sexual abuse.

So, why would your child not talk to you about any of the above problems? The reasons are numerous and here are some that I have heard over the years: "My parents would go ballistic", "I'd be too embarrassed", "My parents wouldn't understand", "My parents would get involved directly and only make matters much worse", "My parents would blame me", "My parents would be too embarrassed" and "I would be punished if I told them." I am sure that many parents would not respond like this but many teenagers believe otherwise and while that is the teenager's belief there is a major problem.

A good question to ask yourselves is, "Would our child confide in us irrespective of the issue or the problem?" You should have a good idea of how your children relate to you. Many teenagers tell me that their parents never listen. This may not be fair to the parents but I do believe that parents are not always aware of how they come across to their children. I do not want to repeat myself, but I do wish to emphasise that creating a safe and non-judgemental environment in the home is essential, and once this is in place many of the barriers between parents and children can be removed or at least reduced.

A related issue is that some teenagers are absolutely terrified of the repercussions for them when they do wrong. This should not be the reality for any teenager and parents need to keep everything in perspective in their response to any situation or crisis. It is for this reason that you should always wait until you are calm and have had time to digest your conversation with your child before responding to their problem. In the immediate aftermath of disclosure you should simply reassure your child that you love them and that you will help them.

A final factor to consider is that young people are far more likely to discuss their intentions of suicide with a person of their own age rather than with an adult. The problem is that it is impossible to get an accurate figure for this because young people are often rigid in maintaining confidentiality and never disclose what they actually knew about the intentions of a young person who died by suicide.

Suicide – A Problem for Society?

I believe that a real problem for us as a society is getting the balance right between treating suicide as normal and sensationalising it. Both have their drawbacks. To treat suicide as no big deal gives young people a signal that dying by suicide is normal and an acceptable behaviour. On the other hand, responding to an incident of attempted suicide or suicide in a sensationalised manner – for example, by referring to it as a public disgrace, or saying that it is nothing other than a selfish act, or that it is the easy way out, or that it takes great courage to die by suicide – is likely to only increase the attraction it might have for young people. We should always regard a suicide as a sad waste of a life and while we should be compassionate in our response to it, we should also clearly indicate to our children that dying by suicide is not the way to deal with personal problems. No matter how bad the personal circumstances of an individual are, they are not insurmountable. Every personal problem can be resolved with the support and help of family and friends.

Suicide is probably the last thing that parents want to think about and that is a very natural feeling. However, the reality is that many young people die by suicide every year and more and more children in their early teens are taking their own lives. While I would not advocate that parents should be preoccupied with the problem, it is important that they are always conscious of the possibility of their child having suicidal thoughts or attempting suicide. I am convinced that raising awareness of suicide in society in general and openly discussing it is one of the best ways of reducing the risk of suicide. I accept that it is almost impossible to prevent every suicide in Ireland, but I am equally certain that the more people – parents, teachers, peers – are aware of the risk factors connected to suicide, the greater the chance that those who are suicidal will get the help they need.

10

Sexual Relationships and Sexuality

Sex education is one of the trickiest and most uncomfortable issues for many parents. Once the subject is mentioned a raft of questions, doubts and fears arise: "When should sex education begin?", "How old should the child be?", "What information should I give?", "I don't feel confident or competent to talk to my child on this subject", "I never received any formal sex education myself and I don't know what to say or where to start", "I picked it up as I grew up and my child can do the same" and "It is far too embarrassing a subject to discuss with my child." In addition, some parents believe that once they have explained the 'facts of life' to their child that they have done their part and the rest is up to the schools. Certainly, schools and teachers have a very important role to play in delivering sex education to children but their role should be no more than a supportive one and the lead should be taken by you as the parents. Sex education should definitely not be left exclusively to schools while you opt out. Schools will provide valuable biological information and technical details incorporating sex education to your child, passing on information and details that many parents simply do not have, but parents can provide a different perspective and should have a different method of delivery than the formal classroom. Indeed, one of the problems with leaving the issue entirely to your child's school is that teachers are educating a whole class of children and naturally will not have the time to speak individually to each child. Also, as it is done in a group situation there is little time for clarification of or discussion about any points which your child may not fully understand. Another point to note is that every child is different and some will be more mature and advanced than others of the same age. If you actively play a part in educating your child on sexual matters, you can tailor the information and discussion to your child's maturity and interest levels in a way their teacher cannot. Finally, and just as importantly, the relationship your child has with their teacher is very different to the relationship they have with you.

The ideal situation is that you take the lead role in providing sex education to your child and the school supports you and your child during the process. Educating your child about sex is a process covering the period from birth, through childhood and adolescence, to the late teens and early adulthood. Furthermore, only a small part of the process is related to the giving of information and facts, as important as they are. By far the most significant part of the process is the communication and discussion element and the building of relationships between parents and child. For this reason, let us establish one important fact at the outset – explaining the facts of life to your child does not, by any stretch of the imagination, complete the sex education of your child and is, in fact, no more than a small element of the whole process.

Laying the Foundation – Early Years

Below are a few suggestions that I believe will help you as you start out on this journey. Golden Rule #1 is to make sure from day one, the day your baby is born, that sex and sex education never become taboo subjects. Always approach the subject with the understanding that sex is a normal and natural part of our make-up as human beings, as are our bodies, and once you operate on this basis sex as a subject will never become embarrassing for you or your child. This matter-of-fact stance will prevent barriers from arising when sex-related issues or questions are raised by you or your child. Do not give your child the impression that sex is a dirty subject or that their sexual organs are dirty. As adults we often say things unaware of the potential damage a casual remark can cause. For example, when a small child touches or holds their genitalia our response is often to say "Don't do that, it's dirty" or "That's bold!" Your child will remember this comment and could grow up believing that their sexual organs are dirty. Instead, tell them that touching their genitalia is ok but it is private and should not be done in public. When talking to your child about issues like this I suggest that you treat it the same as a discussion about good manners and civilised behaviour. There are standards of decency that our culture requires of us. So tell your child not to pull up her dress or to pull down his pants in public in the same matter-of-fact way as you would tell your child not to spit or pick their nose in public.

Golden Rule #2 is never tell lies or give false or mislead-ing information to your child. While it might appear to be the easy option when your three-year-old asks "Where did I come from?" to say "The stork dropped you here" or "We found you under a leaf of cabbage", this is not the approach to take. The problem with telling lies is that eventually your child will find out the truth, possibly in a crude manner and probably from another child. From that moment onwards you will have lost credibility and your child will doubt your reliability and truthfulness. Tell your child the truth but only give as much information as they need at that point in time, sufficient for their level of maturity. If faced with this ques-tion, my advice is to tell your child in a simple but truthful way where and how they were created. For a pre-schooler, for example, you could say, "You grew from a little seed and an egg in Mummy's tummy." That is sufficient information at this stage.

As mentioned above, do not be overly influenced by age. The reality is that every child develops and matures at a different rate and some children will be more advanced in certain areas than other children of the same age. For example one child can be three inches taller at, say, age three than their similarly aged cousin or neighbour. Equally, a child of four can have a much bigger vocabulary than another child of four, and so on. The same is true for levels of maturity. For this reason, sex education must be tailored to suit your child and that is why you play such a central role.

Golden Rule #3 is not to bury your head in the sand and hope that over time the issue will resolve itself or to keep putting 'the talk' off until your child is much older. This is a trap many parents fall into – waiting until the right time. Indeed, sometimes your child is ready but you are not. The result is that your child picks up bits and pieces of information from various sources but without structure and context. However, context is vital. Sex education is as much about context as it is about information. In this scenario, by the time you are ready to introduce the subject of sex education your child will have already picked up bits of information from peers or older children, overheard adults discussing sexual-related issues, read material in books or magazines, or browsed the subject on the internet and perhaps believe that they know it all already, and so will very likely dismiss or ignore your efforts.

The best approach is to engage with your child on a continual basis and to have ongoing and relaxed dialogue on the subject. You must take the lead role and treat the sex education of your child as a normal day-to-day task. Once this approach becomes the norm most of the embarrassment and awkwardness will not arise.

One good tactic is to engage your child rather than just answering questions. I do not mean that questions should not be truthfully answered but I am suggesting that you could open up dialogue by asking your child what they think the answer is. This approach will have two major benefits: it will engage your child and open up discussion between you both, and it will give you a great insight into how much your child already knows about a particular issue, where the knowledge or information was acquired and how well your child is coping with and understanding the issue. When your child asks "Where did I come from?" or "Who made me?", one way of responding is by putting the question back to your child – "Where do you think you came from?" or "Who do you think made you?" It is often very tempting to laugh or make fun of your child's answer but I would urge you not to do so and never to make fun of your child in such circumstances. A central dynamic in this whole process is the building of trust between yourself and your child so it is very important that they are taken seriously during all discussions on sex-related issues, irrespective of how innocent their answers or knowledge of the subject might be. Indeed, I would urge you never to embarrass or humiliate your child under any circumstances and not to talk about your child's beliefs or innocence to a third party in the presence or hearing of your child. To do so will very likely undermine their confidence and make open and frank discussion between you both more difficult.

One final point is that you should try not to respond to your child's questions with a very final and definite answer because if you do so you will likely end the dialogue instantly. For example, if your twelve-year-old child asks, "Dad, do you think young people should have casual sex?" and you respond with "No way", such a definite answer is likely to end the discussion. A better approach is to ask your child "Why do you ask?", followed by "What do you think?"

This will open up a discussion and so you will be able to ascertain why the question was asked in the first place and you will get to know your child's understanding of the issue. You can and should give your opinion during the discussion and also the reasons why you hold such a position, but doing this in the context of a discussion is much better that providing short, sharp answers.

Once it becomes normal and routine to have such discussions with your child all elements of sex education can be addressed and your child will get accurate and sensitive information stage by stage in a safe and loving environment. In addition, you will have a great insight into the level of knowledge and understanding your child has in the whole area of sexuality.

Some of you might feel that you do not have adequate knowledge or communication skills to play the lead role in the sex education of your child but I want to reassure you that you are more than capable of fulfilling this role. You do not need to be doctor or a nurse or a biology teacher to be able to provide your child with sex education. Do not worry about the finer details; your child will get all the necessary biological and technical information in school. Your role is very different – it is to help your child to understand the basic process of developing into a caring, loving and capable human being. Do not be afraid to say to your child, "I don't know the answer but I'll find out." Perhaps you could look up the information together on the internet. Few of us have all the answers but I would encourage you to use your own judgement and instincts.

Puberty

By the age of eight, nine or ten, depending on maturity levels, your child should have a good understanding of how babies are made, the role of fathers and mothers in making the baby and how babies are born. Around that age also it is important that you chat to your child about how their body grows and develops. With a boy discuss and explain puberty, his penis and testicles, sexual arousal and erections. With a girl discuss and explain her development including the stages of puberty, her breasts and vagina, and also her period and how her monthly cycle develops and how it will affect her. Again, remember this is all part of a process that has been ongoing from the day your child was born and so it should happen very normally and it will not feel like a big deal.

You should also discuss the physical and other differences between boys and girls. I want to stress how important it is that in this discussion you should never indicate any superiority of one sex over the other or imply that any activity or preference is only for boys or only for girls. Again, little comments can leave lasting marks. For example, when a little boy is crying we should not say "Stop crying, you are acting like a girl" or "Only little girls cry." This leads the boy to believe that he should not cry and can create serious problems later in life. Boys can often suppress their feelings because they feel it is soft and girlish to show emotion. Likewise, when little girls get involved in rough play we should not say things like "You are a real tomboy." This can lead girls to believe that to be tough is wrong and later when they need to be tough they will opt out. Such comments can have many meanings and we should think about what we are saying and most importantly the meaning and message a child can take from them.

Becoming Sexually Active

One of the things that really frightens many parents is the pace of change in the modern world and how young many children are when they become sexually active. Parents are often shocked to hear a twelve- or thirteen-year-old talk about having 'blow jobs' or to hear that children at that age are sexually active. Of course, not all children of that age are sexually active, but a significant number are. The reality is, for good or for bad, the culture in which children grow up today is very different from that of even ten years ago, and there is nothing much you can do about it other than to prepare your child as best you can. As I have already outlined in the discussion on underage drinking and drugs, the age at which children become involved in many of these activities is getting younger and younger, and the same is true of being sexual active. One of the consequences of this new culture is that your child needs to be prepared and ready for this reality from a very early age. It is much better to ensure your child is prepared and ready to deal with a problem that life throws at them than trying to help them cope in the middle of a crisis. So by the time your child is allowed to attend school discos or other such activities, say fourteen or fifteen years of age, they must be ready to cope with this new and often very challenging environment.

At this age you should talk to your teenager about inter-course, about other sexual activities such as oral sex, about contraception and protected sex, about the dangers of sexual transmitted diseases, about treating other young people with respect and, of course, about having self-respect. Tied into this discussion is one about consent and one about feeling ready. You need to stress to your teenagers the importance of respect for both their partners and them-selves. Teenagers need to aware of the importance of ensuring their partner is fully consenting to sexual activities. If their partner is too drunk to consent, it is rape. If they pressurise their partner into sex, it is rape. Someone does not need to scream or fight back for it to be rape. If they are unsure if their partner wants to engage in sexual acts, they should ask. Consent should not be assumed, it should always be clarified. Similarly, teenagers, both boys and girls, should only be sexually active if they feel ready to. If they do not feel ready they should have the confidence to say no. If they feel they are being pressurised into sexual activity they need to have the self-respect and self-confidence to say no and walk away from the relationship. As their parents, you are the ones who should take the lead in teaching them this and instilling this respect and confidence in them.

I want to stress that not all fourteen- or fifteen-year-olds are sexually active but many are and a child who is not can be put under pressure by someone who is. Again, the issue of maturity comes into play; some children at the age of fourteen will be very developed and mature for their age while others will be very innocent and immature. The best approach is to make sure that your child is well prepared and encouraged to make good choices and not to just go along with the crowd. I fully understand that many parents will be worried about taking away their child's innocence and this is very understandable but if you do not talk to your child about sex and their sexuality then others will and they are far more likely to give misleading and crude information. In addition, you will become removed and isolated from your child's sex education.

The Importance of Boundaries

One important aspect of raising teenagers which ties into this topic is providing them with rules, guidelines and discipline. Like many other areas of your child's development, this too is a process. When your child is a baby all decisions are made by you and this will continue to be the situation for perhaps less than two years. After that your child will gradually become involved in decision-making – "What would you like to eat?", "What would you like to play?" and so on. It is very helpful to have a clear objective during this process and this should be to facilitate your child to grow and develop to their full potential and to become independent, self-sufficient and self-disciplined insofar as possible and to ensure that they are capable of making good, sound decisions and to take full responsibility for them. On the basis of this approach you should plan to allow your child to take control of their life step by step until they are mature and capable of making their own life decisions.

However, children and young people do need controls and boundaries, even if they do not agree with them. I am a strong advocate of parenting on the principle that agreement and consensus is the best approach and I have already given my reasons for this strategy. Nevertheless, during the various stages of your child's development the final say must always rest with you, the parent. What time to go to bed and what time to get up, times of meals, who does what in terms of household chores, time allowed for sport and recreation, time on computers and the access they are allowed, permission to attend concerts, permission to stay overnight with friends, and the amount of pocket money they receive are just some of the issues that you need to decide or at the very least have the final say in. Your child needs security, structure, routine and consistency in their life and they must learn how to be responsible because doing as they wish when and how they decide is not an option.

Why do I discuss this in a chapter dealing with sex education? The reason is that developing personal responsibility, self-discipline and personal control, behaviour limits, and respect for and appreciation of others are all areas linked directly or indirectly to our sexual development and sexuality. I believe that you should always be reasonable, listen attentively to the opinions and views of your child on every issue and try to reach agreement, which on occasions might involve compromise on you or your child's part, but at the end of the day the final decision is yours. You might not feel very happy with the decision you make and your child could be very angry and upset but it is your responsibility and making tough decisions about your children is seldom popular or easy. You must not give in to your child's tantrums, angry outbursts or manipulation efforts because if you do your child will learn that misbehaving and manipulation pays off. During all stages of their childhood and into their teenage years your strategy should be to gradually reduce your control over your child by allowing them more and more personal autonomy. It is all about balance. On the one hand, if you try to control your child's every movement until they leave home they will never learn how to take personal control, will never become independent and will likely become dependent on you. On the other hand, if you have a laissez-faire approach your child will run amuck and have no security or boundaries.

Let me give you an example of what I mean. Your fifteen-year-old daughter asks to stay overnight with her best friend. You say, "Well fine, but I am going to check with your friend's mum to see is it ok and to confirm that they will be at home for the night." It is very likely that your daughter will not want you to do this and will protest, but you should go ahead and check so as to ensure that everything is in order. The big danger with this type of request is that the parents of your daughter's friend are away for the night and the house would become a 'free gaff' – the name given to a house where the parents are absent. When you have confirmation that everything is in order it is safe to allow your daughter to have an overnight stay. Now, let us move on two years; your daughter is now seventeen and she makes the same request. At this stage I feel that circumstances have changed. Assuming that your daughter has been acting responsibly, then you should just talk to her about the potential dangers of a 'free gaff', listing alcohol and drugs as two serious issues, and ask her to be careful and if she has any problems during the night to call you. At seventeen your child is old enough to go away to third-level college and is almost an adult so you will have to begin to trust her.

Sex Abuse and Pornography

One very delicate aspect of sex education is talking to your child about issues like sex abuse, rape, pornography, promiscuity, paedophilia and child abuse. As before, you should do this on an ongoing basis, only giving the amount of information suitable for your child, depending on their development and maturity levels. This is also a very tricky balancing act; on the one hand you want to make sure that your child is protected and aware of the dangers they might face from an early stage of life, but on the other hand you do not want your child to be frightened of or paranoid about other people. The key is to maintain a good balance. From an early age you should talk to your child about not speaking to strangers, not accepting sweets or other items from strangers, not getting into a car or taking a lift from strangers, not going into houses or secluded places with strangers and ensuring they tell you if anything unusual or strange ever happens or is suggested to them by other people. The focus is on maintaining good open communication and making sure to stress that if anything ever did happen it is not your child's fault and you will not be angry with them. This assurance is very important because children are often afraid to tell their parents about bad or dangerous incidents or experiences they had because they are afraid their parents will be angry with them.

As your child develops and matures you must discuss and share more details with them about all of the above issues. The more innocent the child, the more at risk they are and certainly by the age of nine or ten years your child should have a good understanding of what sex abuse is, what rape is and what is generally classified as child abuse. You must create and sustain an environment in which your child will feel safe and secure to confide in you at all times and on all subjects and worries they have during childhood. In order to do so they must have the vocabulary and the understanding to be able to recognise good and bad behaviour. That will be your child's best protection.

Pornography

Pornography, or porn as it is more commonly called, is a subject that you must talk to your children about. It should be discussed on an ongoing and phased basis, linked to the age and maturity level of your child. It is, of course, another issue where getting the proper balance is vital. Some parents might themselves be very innocent regarding porn and never have looked at a pornographic magazine or film, and might even believe that only weird or dirty people look at such material. Others will have seen a lot of porn during their lives and indeed might still be regular viewers. You should accept that porn is widely available in today's world, including Ireland, and it is almost inevitable that your child will be introduced to or have access to some form of porn by the age of ten or eleven, or perhaps even younger.

What exactly is porn? Porn is pictures, images, photographs, videos, books, magazines, films or other material that is intended to arouse sexual excitement. One common example is the 'Page 3 Girl' – a full-page photograph of a topless woman published in many tabloid newspapers. The internet is full of websites which contain all levels and forms of pornographic material, and there are numerous magazines widely available in newsagents that contain porn. The point I want to make is that your child is likely to be exposed to porn material from a relative early age so it is much better to prepare them for the experience rather than to ignore it and leave them much more vulnerable when they are introduced to it or when they come across it, often by accident. Educating your child to know and understand what porn is all about is an essential part of sex education and you should be open and frank about it. Once again, it is important to get the balance right; you should not give your child the impression that their sexual organs are dirty or disgusting but equally you should educate them to respect their bodies, including their sexual organs. It is also a good subject from which to develop discussions with your child around the whole area of the exploitation of people and how some people are forced into this type of behaviour, for instance posing topless or nude, because of their personal or financial circumstances, while others do it out of personal choice.

A related issue is that of child pornography and again you must talk to your child about this matter. You must explain why a child should never allow another person, young or old, to take videos or photographs of any of their sexual organs or when they are in a compromised position, such as with their dress up or trousers down. Again, the emphasis should be on protecting their privacy and having personal respect and not giving the impression that parts of their bodies are dirty. You should stress the dangers of modern technology and how easily sexual images can be flashed around the world with horrific consequences for victims.

Finally, while you have every right to share your own attitude towards (adult) porn with your child you should not adopt a totally dictatorial approach by refusing to discuss it with your child or to listen to their views, especially once your child reaches teenage years. The objective should be to prepare and educate your child to clearly understand what porn is about and to equip them on how to deal with it. It will be absolutely impossible for you to prevent your child getting access to various levels of porn and it is very likely that the more you try to suppress access the more determined your child will be to check it out.

Legal Issues

While I have referred above to modern culture and the fact that many children as young as thirteen or fourteen are sexually active, including having intercourse, it is important that you and your child are aware that the legal age of consent to have intercourse in Ireland is seventeen years of age; this applies to both boys and girls, and to both heterosexual and homosexual sex. Girls are not normally prosecuted for having sex under this age but a small number of boys have been. Having sex with someone under the age of seventeen is a criminal offence known as defilement; it is also often called statutory rape. Your child should be made aware of this because if they are having intercourse with another person, male or female, under the age of seventeen they could be prosecuted.

Religious Beliefs and Sex

A rather complex issue for parents is tying their religious or moral beliefs and the teachings of their church into practical discussions of sex and sexual behaviour. You do, of course, have the right to pass on your beliefs to your children and this is an important aspect of parenting for many people, but I believe that you need to take a practical and realistic approach to this issue. You should make it clear to your child that your religious teaching requires them to behave in a certain manner. However, you also need to acknowledge that many young people will still engage in sexual activities and so be practical about your responsibilities to inform your children. For example, the Catholic Church teaches that engaging in any sexual activity outside of marriage is wrong. You should explain this and any other rules of your belief system that cover sexuality to your child, emphasising that these are the rules of your church and the reasoning behind them. This can form part of the sex education of your child and be incorporated into it at all stages. However, you cannot ignore the fact that many young people will engage in sexual activities, including having full sex outside of marriage, and also many teenagers do not accept the teachings or rules of their parents' religious belief systems. You have a responsibility, therefore, to ensure your children have a comprehensive sex education so that they can make informed decisions. While promiscuity may be against your religious beliefs, you can and should discuss the whole issue of sex and sexuality from two perspectives, both abiding by the teaching of your religion and from an educational, human, cultural and informational level. Otherwise, your child will not be well prepared for the challenges presented by modern youth culture. It is much better to prevent a crisis by being proactive than to have to respond to one.

Relationships

Finally, the foundation on which everything in this chapter is built is good, positive and healthy relationships. The whole process of sex education is very dependent on you having a good, open and relaxed relationship with your child. When relationships are solid then communication, dialogue, discussion and disagreements can be managed successfully and amicably. Throughout this book the skill of listening to your child is highlighted time and time again. Listening is not just about nodding your head and using your ears or going through the motions. Listening is much more than that; it is a skill needing constant attention and development. Good listening involves your ears, eyes, mind and heart – you must hear the words been spoken, read your child's body language, analyse what your child is saying, try to understand what is being said, feel the emotion of your child – the hurt and anger – and see and feel what is going on in your child's life at that particular time. A good listener will know what is not being said as much as what is being said and can help their child to have the confidence, and courage on some occasions, to open up.

Good relationships are based on trust, and building trust can take a long time. One of the amazing things about trust is that it takes a very long time to be built up but it can be destroyed in a matter of seconds; one mistake can destroy trust and end a good relationship. In addition to trust, other important elements in developing and sustaining good relationships are respect for the other person, tolerance, patience, give and take, empathy, generosity, kindness, being non-judgemental and demonstrating the capacity to forgive. The most essential element of all, however, is confidentiality. Few, if any, relationships can be sustained unless both sides maintain strict confidentiality. Any breach of confidentiality will instantly damage and undermine relationships. It is important to stress, therefore, that sex education should include regular references to the importance of relationships in your child's life, and, in particular, the role that relationships play in sexual activities.

It is important that as your child grows they come to understand the difference between having casual sex and having sex in an intimate and loving relationship. As I have stated already, the culture in which your child is growing up is a much changed and generally more liberal culture to the one that existed even five or ten years ago and some children are sexually active from as young as twelve or thirteen years of age, including having sexual intercourse. For this reason it is necessary to discuss with your child the many broader issues linked with and connected to their sexual activity and emphasise that sex is not exclusively a physical experience. One very important element of your child's sexual activity is the context in which it takes place and the relationship that exists with their sexual partner. When it is a once-off experience with a partner where no relationship is in existence then the sexual experience will be shallow and has the potential to damage your child emotionally. In addition, in the absence of a relationship there may be little respect shared or reciprocated by either partner, and one or both can easily be hurt or exploited. The hurt is often caused by the reputation that the young person will inevitable get if they are having regular casual sex with strangers, because that is what it really means if there is no relationship dimension to the sexual act. And regretful and unfair as it is, the reality is that girls suffer much more damage in this regard than boys. A girl will often get the name of being a 'slut', a 'ride' or a 'good thing' while a boy will be regarded as 'spreading his wild oats'. Once a girl gets the reputation of being 'easy to lay' or being sexually liberal then some boys will exploit this and she will find herself under regular pressure to engage in sexual activity, including sexual intercourse. In the interests of balance, I will also point out that boys can be put under pressure by girls to engage in sexual activities like oral sex.

You should discuss with your teenage child the dangers attached to regular casual sex – unwanted pregnancy, sexually transmitted diseases, emotional pain and feelings of being used. Sex carries a lot of emotional baggage and teenagers can often find themselves feeling used or heartbroken if things do not pan out as they expected after they engage in sexual intercourse. This applies equally to boys and girls.

As part of your chats with your teenager child, you should discuss the benefits of having a loving, caring and established relationship with a partner as a prelude to sexual activity, especially intercourse. Keep in mind that this will be regarded as old-fashioned by some young people and they will argue that sex is for pleasure and excitement, that relationships will develop over time and that sexual activity will help form and develop a relationship rather than hinder it. Do not try to force your opinion on your child as this will most likely end discussion on the matter; it is far better to promote the value and meaning of a loving relationship and explain why sexual activity within a loving relationship has much more value and meaning to it than sexual activity in isolation. Highlight the fact that a loving relationship is an essential prerequisite to your child's physical and emotional enjoyment of sexual activity and that sexual intercourse is the most intimate and powerful way for two people to demonstrate and reciprocate their love for each other.

Finally, it goes without saying that not all young people are promiscuous and many never have any sexual activity outside of a loving relationship. If this is the case, you should compliment your child for holding such personal values and principles.

Sexuality

Intimately tied into sex education is the dimension of sexuality. The whole issue of sexuality and sexual orientation should be discussed with your child from around the age of nine onwards, depending on their maturity level. In Chapter 5 I mentioned the fact that boys are often bullied by being called 'queers', 'gay' or 'bent' and that some boys find this very hurtful and offensive. One of the best ways of counteracting this behaviour is to explain to your child in very simple terms the different sexual orientations of people, emphasising that every person, young and old, has the right to their own sexual orientation and that this is completely acceptable in our society. You should explain what being heterosexual means and why it is often referred to as being 'straight'. Also, what being bisexual is and how some people are attracted to both sexes. You should discuss how this can cause a lot of confusion for both boys and girls, particularly as they are growing, and to stress that this is a normal stage of development. You should discuss what being gay, lesbian or homosexual means and what 'coming out' means. You should not stigmatise, laugh at or sneer at any sexual orientation, and most definitely you should not condemn any group. This is a very sensitive time for many young people and you must treat it as such.

In Chapter 4 I dealt with what I call 'accepting the reality of your child', but I must revert to it here because the whole issue of sexuality can raise many difficult and very sensitive challenges for both you and your child. How do you respond if and when your child tells you that they are gay or bisexual? Again, if you are having regular and ongoing chats with your child it is very unlikely that they will shock you by mentioning an issue like their sexual orientation out of the blue. This is one of the central reasons why I recommend that you have ongoing and open dialogue with your child about their sexuality and sexuality in general from an early age. If you are having such dialogue it will soon become normal for you and your child to touch upon this subject and for you and your child to express your views and feelings. It will also be much easier for you to respond openly and confidently when the sexual orientation of your child is being discussed.

However, one of the biggest problems for parents arise when there is no dialogue or communication on sexuality and then out of the blue you become aware of the fact that your child is gay, lesbian or bisexual either from your own observations or from another source, or your child suddenly confides in you. In such circumstances parents often react with shock, disappointment, embarrassment and, in some cases, anger. By expressing such feelings and showing such a reaction you will certainly make it very difficult, if not impossible, for your child to continue to confide in you. You should not respond by saying things like "You are not one of them", "What is wrong with you?", "I thought you were normal", "I'll get you help" or "Ah, you will grow out of it", or give any indication whatsoever that your child is anything other than normal. Of course for many parents the fact that their child has a sexual orientation that they would regard as not the norm can be a shock. They will be concerned about their child's future and may have fears about issues like having a family, getting married or the dangers of being picked on or bullied.

Nevertheless, this is certainly a situation where your unconditional love must come into play and you must freely and generously indicate to your child that you are there to provide love and support and that your only interest is helping your child to be happy and contented with their life. A hug would go a long way in communicating and demonstrating your love and support at times like this. While Irish society has progressed over the past decade or so, it is still very difficult for a person, young or old, to openly and publicly declare their sexual orientation if it is different to what is culturally the norm. It takes great courage for your child to even talk about their feelings and sexual orientation and you should be sensitive in how you respond. The best reaction is to listen to what your child has to say and not to put any pressure on them or try to force your child to say more than they are comfortable with at that time. Later on you can talk to your child about how you feel and how you intend to deal with the issue, but always indicate full support for your child. You can also suggest to your child that they make contact with various support groups that provide excellent advice and support for young people who are gay, lesbian or bisexual.

The same advice holds true for more complex issues, such as if your child declares that they are transgender or if they have an intersex condition. Such complex issues cannot be discussed in detail in this book but they should be dealt with with sensitivity, tact, openness and understanding.

A Final Word

The sex education of your child is very important and the earlier you start the better. Of course, there will be occasions when it will be trying, difficult and even embarrassing, but you are the best person to lead this process. The world your child is now living in is a very different world to when you were a child or a teenager, and this applies even if you are still in your twenties. Your child needs you to be their guide in this complex and confusing place.

11

Sport and Recreational Activities

Sport and recreational activities are essential elements in the development of all healthy children and so parents should encourage participation in such activities. It is vital that you regard sport and recreational activities primarily as fun enjoyment opportunities for your children. Sport has many positive benefits for young people. Most sports are played outdoors and as a result provide young people with plenty of fresh air. Many sports involve physical effort and again this is healthy for the child. Parents might be surprised at how physically unfit many young children are in today's world. The car and school bus have replaced walking and cycling to a large extent, and today many children do not walk to or from school, and they do not walk or cycle to the football field or the swimming pool. There are many good reasons for this, such as child safety, but the reality is that many children do very little physical exercise. In addition, many of the old games and activities like hopscotch and skipping are seldom played nowadays. Instead, large numbers of children sit at home playing games on their computer or watching television. So sport has the potential to compensate for this. We also know that child obesity is a huge problem in the modern world and while physical exercise on its own is not the complete answer to this phenomenon, it certainly helps.

One of the great scourges of modern life is that almost every activity has a competitive element to it and winning is the only thing that seems to count. This problem is discussed more below, but I am convinced that many parents, often unintentionally, actually ruin their child's enjoyment of sport because of their emphasis on 'winning'. Instead, parents should simply encourage their children to play sport or try other recreational activities because it is enjoyable. I would urge you not to force or overly influence your children towards any single sport or activity but let them discover for themselves what they enjoy most. Allow your child to try every sport and recreational activity available to them in your locality. Over time they will develop a liking for some sports over others. For example, some children will love contact sports, while others will love non-contact sports. Some will like team sports while others will prefer individual sports. The best-known contact sports are team sports such as Gaelic football, hurling, soccer, rugby, hockey, camogie and ladies football, and while boxing is very much an individual sport, it is, of course, a physical contact sport. Some of the most popular non-contact sports are tennis, basketball, handball, volleyball, athletics, gymnastics, swimming, horse riding, cycling, bowling, golf and rowing. You should encourage your children to try their hand at all types of sports as they usually provide very different rewards and experiences.

The Benefits of Playing Sport

Apart from the health benefits of taking exercise and being in the fresh air, sports of all types provide many benefits to your child. Team sports help to develop team work and team spirit; the individual must be prepared to be a team player and most of the satisfaction will come from being part of a team rather than from personal performance. I am not saying that one does not get personal gratification from team sports but the overriding satisfaction comes from being part of a team. Team sports provide wonderful learning opportunities for children in many different ways, such as developing self-discipline, leadership, team work and team spirit, and having respect for fellow team members and opponents, match officials and supporters. In addition, team sports help to develop a sense of camaraderie, improve self-esteem, build confidence, create friendships that can last for a lifetime and teach children about winning and losing. Children can also develop many social skills such as taking instructions. Above all, they experience fun and enjoyment when participating in team sports. It is not surprising therefore that I rate team sports very highly and I would certainly urge you to encourage your children to participate in some team sports from an early age simply to enable them to experience the many positive outcomes outlined above.

Individual and non-contact sports also have many benefits for your child; they will help your child to develop certain skills and competencies, including many of those already discussed above, and this in turn will build confidence and self-esteem. Individual sports require your child to be dedicated, committed and disciplined just as much as many contact and team sports.

A key benefit of individual sports is helping your child to develop self-discipline. For example, unlike many team sports where training takes place in groups under the direct supervision of coaches or mentors, many individual sports will require your child to practise on their own. This is where self-disciple becomes a key requirement – they will often have to get up early in the morning and spend many hours a week training and practising various skills, usually without direct supervision. During periods of active involvement in the particular sport sticking to the proper methods and approaches – including sometimes such elements as strict diets – is vital and depends greatly on your child's self-discipline. Self-discipline is also an important element of team sports as children must learn to follow the rules and play in their team's best interests. Self-discipline, therefore, is a crucial attribute for participation in all sports and it is a quality that will be of immense value to your child in and outside sport and throughout life.

There are many benefits from playing sports, both team and individual, contact and non-contact. One wonderful benefit is that your child will soon realise the need for personal endurance, total commitment and, on many occasions, personal sacrifice. The message must be clear and simple – if you want to be a high achiever at any sport you must work hard. But do remember that this should be your child's choice and decision rather than yours. If a child's commitment is driven by a personal interest in and a love and passion for the sport or activity, then it is very likely that it will become a life-long interest. However, when it is forced on the child by a domineering parent the child will hate the activity and will opt out at the first opportunity. Your objective, as parents, should be to pass on a love and passion for sport or other recreational activities, not to force your child to do something they do not enjoy.

Sport is excellent for helping children to realise and value the importance of preparation. Sport is one area where preparation is vital and without it very little will be achieved. To quote Roy Keane, 'fail to prepare, prepare to fail.' Using the example of sport, it is easy to communicate to your children that this maxim equally applies to many other areas of their lives.

Sport also promotes other values such as honesty; this applies particularly in team sports where all members must pull their weight and play for the team rather than themselves. Team sports help to develop bonding amongst teammates. Young people become aware of the importance of dependability – each player depends on their fellow teammates to perform and each takes personal responsibility for the overall good of the team. There is also a strong emphasis placed on the honour and integrity of the individual sportsperson in many individual sports. For example, golf is often referred to as a sport of 'honour' as individual players are expected to play and abide by the rules as a matter of honour. Golf players have many opportunities to cheat but it is a sport based on the integrity of the players. Your child will benefit from this type of environment and philosophy and will learn to recognise a cheat or cheating behaviour.

Finally, sport is great for facilitating children to set targets or goals for themselves and their team. The coach will introduce a skill and demonstrate it and then ask the children to practise it between coaching sessions. This is an ideal way of getting children to recognise the importance of putting in hard work to succeed. Once they have conquered a skill, their coach will tell them that they have achieved their target and so they will be able to connect hard work and personal dedication with achievement. This is also an ideal opportunity for you to support and encourage the efforts of your child. Skills practice can be very frustrating and at times even boring; just repeating the same skill or perhaps trying to conquer a new skill is by far the most difficult part of sport. The many long hours that your child will spend practising are often not recognised. A few words of encouragement and a bit of praise will be greatly appreciated by your child on occasions like this. Spending time with your child during practice is also time well spent; just being there is so important. However, do not criticise and only interfere or get involved if and when your child asks for your help; your job is to encourage, encourage, encourage. A survey of many of America's top female tennis players found that almost all the players wanted their parents to be there to provide a shoulder to cry on, to listen to their moans, to encourage them and to let them give out about their coaches and let off steam. They did not want them to be their coaches and they did not want them to criticise their performance. Your child will have to listen to their coach criticising them; they need their parents to be parents.

Unwilling Participants

I want to emphasise, however, that you should only encourage and not force your children to participate in sports. Some children are very shy and hate to be placed in an awkward situation where they feel unhappy and uncomfortable. This is not going to help your child develop self-confidence and your child will not enjoy the experience. You should also accept that some children simple hate physical contact sports and if this is the case for your child do not force the issue. Often parents who themselves were or indeed still are active in sports expect their children to follow in their footsteps and some parents cannot understand why their child has no interest in sports. Some then resort to either forcing their child to participate or else continuously nagging their child about their refusal to do so. Neither approach is effective. Your child will resent you if you push them into participating, and constant nagging will damage both your child's self-confidence and the quality of your parent–child relationship. It is my experience that fathers are more likely to be guilty of this approach than mothers.

Competitiveness and Sportsmanship

To return to a point I made at the start of this chapter, I have no hesitation in saying that competition and competiveness are introduced much too early into the sporting lives of too many children. Indeed, many parents believe that being competitive in sport will help their children to realise that life itself is very competitive and the sooner they learn this, the better they will be prepared for life. I completely disagree with this philosophy as I believe that introducing children to competitiveness at a very young age is far more likely to damage the child than to be helpful. Once competition is introduced then the only thing that really matters is winning and much of the fun and enjoyment of participation will be lost. In addition, the whole selection process, especially in team sports, will focus on winning and only the most skilled and physically strong children will be selected to play, leaving many children sitting on the sidelines, feeling rejected and believing themselves to be failures. This is an example of where sport can be destructive rather than constructive in the development of children. One of the great tragedies of the modern attitude to sport is the over-emphasis on winning; instead of sport being a relief from the day-to-day pressure of life it all too often has become nothing more than an added pressure on young people. Sport must be seen as providing a break for children from school and study, and something that the child enjoys and looks forward to rather than just another activity. I strongly urge you to allow your children plenty of time to learn and develop the various skills of each sport without a competitive element; the more skill your child develops the more enjoyment they will get from the sport. The emphasis, therefore, should be on technique and skills development rather than competition and winning. Of course, I am not opposed to competitiveness completely but there is a time and a place for it and I do not believe it is appropriate for children under the age of twelve. At around this age, children will have developed the basic skills of many sports and will be able to choose which ones they prefer.

When the time comes to introduce your child to competitive sport they will learn how to win and how to lose. Both experiences are vital to your child's development. I am never happy when I read about an underage team in any sport or activity that is unbeaten for a long period of time. This not a good experience for the players, no more than it is for a team of young people to always be beaten. Children need to experience both winning and losing. Parents should be aware of the significance of both experiences and what the appropriate behaviour should be. When your child is part of a winning team or wins as an individual they should learn to be humble in victory and to respect those who are on the losing side. Equally important, your child can learn from defeat by acknowledging that their opponents were better on the day and to accept defeat graciously.

I must now return to the whole issue of winning. I have personally witnessed adults, including the parents of the children competing, mainly fathers, shouting at them to foul an opponent and to behave in an unsporting manner, encouraging them to win at all costs. Parents should never behave in such a manner and they should never encourage children to be unsporting. Children should be encouraged to play by and within the rules at all times, to fully accept the decisions of referees and match officials, and to accept when they are beaten by a more skilled opponent. The late and great Dermot Earley wrote a lovely piece about this in a book called *A Just Society*, edited by John Scally:

"Forty years ago, I played a juvenile game in the west of Ireland that was a close, hard-fought contest. My immediate opponent was a top-class player and I still remember the contest as we tried to better one another. Towards the end of the game, I broke clear and headed for goal. My opponent gave chase and put me under pressure. As I got closer to the posts, a coach from the opposing team roared continuously, 'Pull him down, pull him down.' Under pressure, I got my shot away and scored. As I jogged back outfield with my opponent close by, the coach roared, 'Why didn't you pull him down?' My opponent stopped running and in a pleading voice and arms outstretched, he calmly said, 'That's not how you play football.'"

Sport and Study

When children get older and, for example, they are in their final year in secondary school, studying for the Leaving Certificate, some parents pressurise their children to opt out of sport during that period. I disagree with this approach. Indeed, I firmly believe sport has a special and positive role to play at this stage of a child's life. As I have emphasised repeatedly in this chapter, sport should be an enjoyable and relaxing activity for children. I believe that getting away from study for a few hours a week to play sport is actually very therapeutic for the young person and that as a result the quality of your child's study will be improved rather than hindered. Some parents will be concerned that their child might get injured and perhaps break a finger or arm. My response is that this could happen in the house or on the street, and little good will be achieved by wrapping your child up in cotton wool. Studying for exams is likely to be stressful for your child. It is also very demanding emotionally and psychologically, and having a break from it for a few hours a week helps to reduce the pressure. Sport provides the ideal opportunity for this. Of course, it is important to get the balance right between study and sport. Sport should be seen as recreational and study as work. All play and no work is just as bad as all work and no play – the key is balance.

Other Recreational Activities

The principles that I have outlined in relation to participation in sport also apply to other recreational activities such as dancing, art, drama and music. Encourage your children to try them out, again just for enjoyment reasons. Many children are forced to participate in many of the creative arts and because of this they grow to hate and resent them rather than to enjoy and love them. Just as with sport, in dancing or music it is too often about winning competitions rather than dancing or playing for enjoyment. Sometimes, however, the creative arts are looked down upon and some parents believe that children should not be wasting their time with them. This is absolute nonsense and I strongly believe that the creative arts have unlimited potential for both the enjoyment and development of children.

'Thinking outside the box' is a modern motto but how well prepared are our children for this new requirement? In actual fact, most of their everyday lives are structured and lived inside a box. The creative arts will provide your child with the opportunity to be innovative and creative and to interpret the world in their own individual way. Children generally love to perform and exhibit their work and the creative arts facilitate this in many ways. They enable children to communicate their views, ideas and experiences in their own unique way. I love the little story about the six-year-old girl in America published in Ken Robinson's book *The Element*:

"An elementary school teacher was giving a drawing class to a group of six-year-old children. At the back of the classroom sat a little girl who normally didn't pay much attention in school. In the drawing class she did. For more than twenty minutes, the girl sat with her arms curled around her paper, totally absorbed in what she was doing. The teacher found this fascinating. Eventually, she asked the girl what she was drawing. Without looking up, the girl said 'I'm drawing a picture of God.' Surprised, the teacher said, 'But nobody knows what God looks like.' The girl said 'They will in a minute.'"

I love this story as it really summarises the innocence, creativity, self-confidence and imagination of little children. It is my experience and belief that children are naturally very creative, but the reality is that it is us adults who play the biggest part in knocking these wonderful qualities and beliefs out of our children. Much of our educational system restricts this creativity rather than supports it. We must remember that happy children are confident children and anything that helps this should be encouraged. That is one of the main reasons why I am a strong fan and advocate of the creative arts as they facilitate individuality in a good and positive way and they encourage and enable children to be different in a culture that pressurises young people to all be the same.

Music also has wonderful benefits for your child and you should encourage them to have a go at it. Not every child has musical talent and ability, so if your child does not do not fret. However, your child does not have to be a musical genius to enjoy music or to be encouraged to take it up. It is a wonderful gift for your child to have a talent in and you should talk to your child about its potential, but do not force the issue. A relatively cheap musical instrument like a recorder or a tin whistle will establish the musical ability and interest of your child. Do not invest in an expensive musical instrument until such time as you are satisfied that your child has some musical talent and also an interest in learning music. You should also introduce your child to a wide range of music and not confine them to classical music, a genre that some children love and others hate.

Like sport, some children love the performing and competitive element of music and others have no interest in this aspect. If your child does not like performing, even within the family, then do not force the issue. Your priority should be to encourage your child to enjoy music as an activity; everything else is a bonus. Some parents push their children to perform publicly just to show them off and to boast about how wonderful they are while ignoring the feelings of their children. Do not be this person.

Finally, in addition to the great benefits that music has as an activity and as an educational subject, it also has a therapeutic dimension to it. When your child is tired of study, bored or just fed up or browned off, music will often prove to be their saviour; your child will sit at the piano or pick up a musical instrument and immerse themselves in a piece of music, so that all their stresses melt away.

12

Fathers

I decided to write a chapter aimed specifically at fathers because, while the role of fathers has changed very significantly over the past twenty years or so, many fathers are still missing out on some of the most wonderful and exciting events in their children's lives. Some fathers now work full-time as house husbands or stay-at-home dads and are fully involved in the rearing of their children, but I think it is still fair to say that most fathers work outside the home and their job accounts for a big portion of their day-to-day life. While many of these fathers play a strong and active role in their children's lives, for many others they would prefer to spend their free time playing golf or socialising in the pub rather than spending time with their children. This chapter is aimed particularly at this group of fathers.

The Role of Fathers

Fathers are hugely important in the lives of children and I do not think that many people would disagree that the ideal situation for children is to have both a loving mother and a loving father caring for them during their childhood and into their teenage years. Of course, this is not always the reality and many children are reared in loving environments by one-parent families or other variations such as two-mother or two-father families, stepfamilies or by their grandparents or other guardians with absolutely no difficulties. However, I believe that fathers and mothers play very different roles in their children's lives and both roles are of equal importance to the child's development. Many fathers still see their main role as the breadwinner for their family and they devote a huge part of their lives to work, and as a direct result their input into their children's early lives is minimal. Personally I would say to fathers to make sure that you regard your job as just that – a job. While of course your job is very important, it must never be allowed to take over your life to the detriment of your children's development and enjoyment. Few people on their death bed regret not working longer and harder during their life, but I am sure many fathers regret not spending more time with their children, especially when they were young.

Spending Time with Your Child

The more I observe children in today's world the more I am convinced that parents have a very limited time when they are wanted by their children – I would say about fourteen years at most. From then on the shoe is on the other foot and it is parents who are competing for their children's attention, and they often struggle to get it. Once they become teenagers, children will only pay attention to their parents when they want to and not when the parents require it. This is something that most fathers never realise until it comes to pass, and then it is too late and many subsequently regret the lost opportunities. My message to fathers, therefore, is to have as few regrets as possible by making sure that your work and other commitments are balanced against spending quality time with your children during those early years. On the day our first child was born, an old friend of mine told me to read aloud to her. I said, "I will when she gets bigger", and he replied "No, not when she gets bigger. Do it now." I am sure that many dads would feel like I did, that a baby only a few days old would not understand or be interested in listening to an adult reading a story. However, I am now convinced that fathers should talk and read to their baby from day one as it is very therapeutic for both father and baby and it definitely helps fathers bond with their children. Indeed, fathers should participate in every single activity in their baby's care and development, including changing nappies, bathing, and so on. Of course, many fathers do so but many others do not, and they lose out in the long term.

As a father, you should organise plenty of fun days and times with your children. Children will always remember the fun days with their parents, and they do not have to be very expensive outings – walking in the countryside, playing sport, going on picnics, cycling, go to sporting occasions and even just going for a stroll can be fun for child and parent. You should remember the short few years that your children want you to be around – if you are there when they want you, they might listen to you when they are older.

Be There for Your Child

No matter how busy you are, as a father you should make sure that you are present as much as possible for most of the important times and events in the early stages of your child's life. When I say 'present', I mean physically, mentally and emotionally – there no use being there if you are not paying attention to your child; do not stand on the sidelines checking your email on the phone. I know some fathers who say, "Ah when he's bigger I'll play football with him and I'll take him to matches." Promises, promises, promises – the reality is that this seldom happens. Time flies and before you know it your child will no longer need their father's presence or attention. My advice to fathers is to grab the opportunities when they are there and accept that they will not last forever.

Put the important dates in your diary and just make sure to be there; your job will wait. All the firsts in a child's life are not to be missed by both parents if at all possible – the first time going to crèche, going to school, first school play, sporting occasions like first match, first dancing competition, and so on. The thing to remember is that all firsts are one-off occasions and will never be repeated. If they are missed they are gone forever. I am often amazed at the absolutely rubbish reasons fathers put forward to justify their absence from important events in their children's lives – "I forgot all about it", "I was too busy in the office", "The traffic was very heavy and I felt I would not make it in time", "I was on my way but I ran into an old mate from college and we went for a pint", "I know nothing about football but I'll go next time" or "It was raining and I had no coat."

Of course it is not possible for parents to be present on every occasion and event in their children's young lives but the reality is that mothers generally make it their business to be there, while many fathers make excuses. Too many fathers live to regret the many significant occasions in their child's life that they were 'too busy' to attend. Of course you will not be able to get off work on every occasion, but this should be the exception rather than the norm.

Discipline

Fathers should not set out to be the 'tough parent' or the one who only intervenes when issues of discipline arise. Some fathers almost relish the role of disciplinarian, believing that this is one of their main responsibilities. Of course promoting and encouraging children to have a good understanding of self-discipline is very important and you should regard discipline as a positive and normal part of your child's development. You should explain why disciple is important and why controls and boundaries apply to all people, irrespective of age, and discuss these issues and any questions your children have with them. I cannot emphasise enough the importance of explaining the reasons why self-discipline is so crucial in all our lives. Disciple and self-discipline are often seen as the same but they are actually very different – disciple is usually imposed on one person by another while self-discipline is nourished from within the person. Disciple must not be a means of enforcing rules and controls on children but a means of educating and promoting self-control; one is a negative experience while the other is a positive one. Fathers and mothers need to understand this crucial difference in their approach to disciple. Obviously, parents themselves should also be good examples to their children when it comes to self-discipline.

The big challenge arises when a child has misbehaved in some way and parents have to intervene. Such interventions should be shared between both parents, irrespective of the seriousness of the misbehaviour. I would strongly suggest that fathers of teenagers should avoid confrontation as much as possible. Some fathers have a habit of directly and often aggressively confronting their teenage children when they misbehave or refuse to obey an instruction. This style of dealing with a problem is doomed to fail and some of the collateral damage has long-term consequences. Fathers should also never use their physical strength to force or intimidate a child. Again, this can lead to serious long-term repercussions. This type of behaviour will damage your relationship with your child and there is also the likelihood that your child will grow to fear you or hate you and they will quickly disengage and disconnect from you. As a result you will become very peripheral to your child's life and your role as a father will be diminished. Ultimately, you will be the biggest loser. I know of many teenagers who have no contact or communication with their fathers because they acted like tyrants when the teenager misbehaved or failed in some way. This approach might win the battle but it is most likely going to lose the war – it will be a case of short-term gain for long-term loss.

The important point is that discipline is not something that should be associated with any type of hard-hearted approach, insensitivity, harshness or cruelty. There are two approaches, soft and hard skills, and I am always on the side of the soft skills. Many fathers believe that discipline can only be enforced by taking a hard-line approach. I actually believe the opposite and that a soft skills approach is much more effective, especially in the long term. To clarify what I mean – using hard skills or taking the hard-line approach is to operate a harsh regime like using force against your child – pushing them to the ground, pinning them against a wall, physically throwing your child into a cot or chair in an angry manner, or using physical punishment like slapping or punching. It also includes verbal abuse like shouting at your child, always sharply criticising them, using bitter and hurtful words of condemnation or criticism, talking down at your child or refusing to listen to your child's side of the story or their opinion. On the other hand, a soft skills approach is when you discuss the problem in a calm manner, you suppress your anger and irritation, and you wait until you have calmed down before dealing with the problem. It is when you explain to your child what the problem is and how it can be resolved or rectified, when you distinguish between your child's behaviour and your child the person, when you encourage rather than condemn, when you listen attentively to your child's side of the story, when you explain why you are imposing some sanction as a punishment, when you show patience and understanding, when you empathise with your child, and when you do not hold grudges. With a soft skills approach you finish on a positive, like, "I know that you are a good boy/girl and that you will do better from now on", "We all make mistakes but we have to learn from them and I know you will" or "That is the end of it now, I have dealt with it and we'll move on." Some people confuse a soft skills disciplinary strategy with being soft on wrongdoing or misbehaviour, or believe that such a strategy is weak and ineffective when it comes to imposing punishment. Nothing could be further from the truth; you can use the soft skills approach and impose whatever punishment you consider appropriate. It is more about how you do it rather than what you do. Believe me, very tough punishments can be imposed using the soft skills approach, but the outcome will be very different. With the hard skills approach your child is likely to feel hurt and disrespected, whereas with the soft skills approach your child will appreciate being treated in a respectful manner and will understand where you are coming from as a father. So, as an example, if your child seriously misbehaves you can withdraw their pocket money for two, three or four weeks using the soft or hard skills approach, but I feel certain that your child will learn much more when you use the soft skills approach. (See Chapter 3 for a further discussion on discipline.)

After disciplining your child, one parent should always be available and be prepared to listen to their child. I want to stress that I am not suggesting one parent should undermine the other, but they should simply provide an ear to allow the child to vent. Teenagers especially must be allowed the opportunity to vent; it is much better than forcing them to suppress their anger and frustration. Most importantly, parents should not get angry and abusive, even when very serious misbehaviour has occurred. The best and most effective way for you, as parents, to manage any incident of misbehaviour is to remain cool and collected at all times. Remember, what is the objective of the disciple process and what outcome do you wish to achieve? Your primary aim should be to help your child to have better self-discipline and not to repeat the misbehaviour. The focus should not be on punishment or 'putting the fear of God' into the child. Again, I am aware of many fathers who go over the top when dealing with their child's misbehaviour, and naturally in the process they seriously damage their relationship with their child. Indeed, many teenagers have told me that they would never be able to approach their fathers about any misbehaviour because of their likely reaction. Comments such as "My dad would go ballistic", "My dad would kill me" or "No way could I talk to Dad; he just loses it every time I do something wrong" are some of the most frequent responses I get from teenagers. Believe it or not, many teenagers, boys and girls, have no relationship whatsoever with their fathers and some say that they never even speak to them. This is a very sad situation for both fathers and children and should never be allowed to reach such a stage. Fathers have the major responsibility to prevent this happening. I must emphasise, the day that communication breaks down between fathers and their children is the day that they have failed as parents. It is a basic as that – if parents cannot communicate with their children they cannot parent.

Parental Love

As discussed in previous chapters, I believe in the importance of chatting regularly to your children, and I would stress to fathers the need to do this. Some fathers chat all the time with their children but others do not, and this is often the case when the children reach teenage years. Some fathers are too strict and just keep on pushing their teenager and seldom, if ever, relax with them. However, if you spend time chatting with your children and doing enjoyable activities with them, such as going for walks and picnics or attending sporting occasions, your child can clearly see your love for them.

Fathers *must* love their children unconditionally. This is often very difficult for some fathers to grasp but it is actually non-negotiable. I would urge you, as a father, never to respond to any problems or difficulties you are having with your children by indicating that your continued love is conditional. Indeed, if and when your child is in difficulty this is the time when unconditional love is most required.

Fathers should tell their children that their love is unconditional, irrespective of the child's achievements or behaviour. Telling your child that your love is unconditional does not mean that you are 'soft' on them or that you cannot therefore discipline your child. Communicating clearly with your child enables them to understand why they are being disciplined, if that is necessary, or why you will not allow them to do certain things (such as going to a nightclub) but still be secure in the knowledge that you love them.

When your child is trying to please you by, for example, telling you how well they did in an exam, it is good to say something like, "That's superb; I'm delighted you did so well, but remember I would equally love you if you had failed your exam." Likewise, when your child makes a mistake or fails to achieve to their ability tell them, "I'm sorry you are disappointed with how you did but I still love you just as much as ever." The point is that a father's love must not be linked to good behaviour or to good achievement; it must be unconditional so just because you have to disciple and punish your child does not mean that you are withdrawing your love from your child. In actual fact, one of the main reasons why we impose limits and restrictions on our children is because we love them and we do not want to see them get hurt or to hurt others.

Accepting Your Child for Who They Are

As discussed in Chapter 4, fathers should accept that every child is different and unique and what works with one child will not necessary work with another. Accepting this reality will go a long way in helping you to appreciate the uniqueness of each child. And, as I have stated already, children should never be compared to one another; they are all different and that is part of the wonder of life.

I would like to mention the whole area of sport again just for the benefit of fathers. Again, this does not apply to all fathers but many fathers are very eager for their children to play sport. I have already dealt with the great benefits of playing sport in Chapter 11 and I would urge fathers to encourage their children to play sport, but if a child is not interested then do not force the issue. Fathers who played sport themselves and loved it often feel that their children should be sporting, and some cannot accept it when their child shows no interest in sport. This sometimes results in the father forcing the child to get involved in sporting activities, creating a disastrous situation where the child grows to hate sport and probably also hate their father for, as they see it, ruining their lives. If your child loves playing sport it's wonderful for both you and your child but if your child has no interest then you should fully accept this and not put any pressure on your child to play sport. Above all, you should not develop a grudge or negative attitude towards your child because of this. You need to be aware that any indication you give to your child that you are not happy with their refusal to play sport can be very damaging psychologically for them. Your child might feel that they have let you down or that they are failures because they do not like sport, and this in turn will damage their self-confidence. As a father, you should totally and unreservedly accept your child's decision and fully respect it and move on with no negative attitude or regrets – once again the emphasis is on fully accepting your child's reality.

13

Measuring Parenting Success

One of the advantages of getting older is that it is much easier to recognise the things that are most important in life. The same is true with parenting; the older you are and the longer you are a parent the more aware you become of the things that really matter in the life of your child and the things that are really important. Unfortunately, it is usually too late for your children by the time you have it all conquered. One realisation you will come to as you become a more experienced parent is that only two things really matter in your child's life, and so I recommend that on a regular basis you ask yourself "Is my child healthy and is my child happy?" These are the only measures of parenting success that really matter; everything else is secondary. When life is stressful and your children are driving you up the wall, just remember this.

The first measurement is the health of your child. This is so simple and basic but still most of us overlook the fact that good health is the greatest gift that any child, or indeed any person, can have in life. This is brought home to us when our children are sick, even with a common illness such as the flu, a cough or measles. Such times remind us that there is a very thin line between good health and sickness. Nursing our children through an illness helps us to appreciate the value and importance of good health and we acknowledge this by saying things like, "I wish you were back on your feet again; I didn't know how lucky I was when you were well." Having a sick child puts things in perspective – tidy rooms and music practice no longer seem so important.

The second measurement is equally simple – a happy child. During my talks I often ask parents, "Is there anything in the world that you would put ahead of the health and happiness of your children?" When put in such stark terms, parents will readily say "No" to this question, but precisely because it is so obvious many parents actually overlook the importance of happiness. I would go so far as to say that it does not get nearly the attention it deserves. The sad truth is that because, as parents, we have convinced ourselves that we know what is best for our children we often actually cause a lot of unhappiness for them. We force them to do things and get involved in activities that they hate because we are driven by a belief that it is for their own good. Now of course young children do not know what is best for them and we must make numerous decisions on their behalf but I believe that as children grow older, say from around six years of age onwards, they should be involved in the decisions that are being made in their interest. As parents we too often decide on a course of action without taking our child's views into consideration. Worse still, if our child offers an opinion we just ignore it. For example, when a child says "I don't like football", their parent might say "Ah you do. You'll get to like it."

The measurement for parenting success is a happy child. However, forcing your child to do something against their will certainly will not contribute to their happiness. I now believe that parents should put 90 per cent of their energy into trying to get their child's agreement and consent and just 10 per cent into enforcement of a decision. If you pass on a love of a particular activity to your child it will remain with them for life. On the other hand, forcing your child to do something they dislike will just damage your relationship and they will drop the activity at the first available opportunity.

I have personal experience of this as a parent and over the years I have come across numerous other examples. In my own case it was forcing my daughters to swim. I never learned to swim and so I decided, in my wisdom, that my daughters would learn to swim from a relatively early age. However, I never asked them; I told them. Every Saturday for a number of years I would instruct them to "Get in the car" and then drove them to the local swimming pool where they learned to swim under the supervision of a qualified instructor. Years later, when I spoke to them about the things they hated most during their childhood, they declared "You ruined every Saturday for us" and told me that they cried every Friday night knowing that the next day they would be forced to go to swimming lessons. They grew up hating swimming. If I was to go back and start all over again as a parent I would handle the whole swimming thing quite differently. I would put my energy into convincing my daughters that swimming is brilliant, pointing out all the wonderful pluses – it's great exercise, it's great recreation, you could save your own life if you ever got caught in high waters and you might save someone else's life if they are drowning. However, if they still showed no interest I would simply say to them, "Fine, do whatever you like – play tennis, football, hockey – whatever you like really, but when you're drowning don't come back and try to blame me." But I would not force them into swimming as I did before.

Unfortunately, my original approach is widespread; young children grow to hate sport, music and many other activities because it too was imposed on them. They seize the first chance they get to quit, leaving parents angry and often out of pocket. The only way to avoid this scenario is to ensure that your child's voice is heard from an early age. Children are much wiser than we give them credit for and if they do not like something it is useless continuing to force them; you are only putting off the inevitable. I am not suggesting that you simply allow your child to give up the first time they hit a bump in the road but rather, as I have argued throughout this book, talk to your child, listen to their perspective and try to reach a consensus. If they want to give up football because of one bad match experience, for example, chat to them about the importance of perseverance and encourage them to keep playing for another few weeks. However, if they genuinely and consistently dislike the activity do not try to force the issue. A simple guide is to observe the difference in your child's behaviour when they are preparing to go to training or practice. If they enjoy the activity it will be obvious. They will be looking forward to going, just as they would if they were going to a birthday party. If they dislike the activity and are going because they have to, again it will be obvious. They will be down in the dumps, quiet on the journey there and, worse still, hating every minute while there. Nothing good or positive is achieved in this situation and your child is suffering rather than enjoying what is supposed to be a fun activity. Of course it is not possible to get the agreement and consent of our children all the time. I do not expect you to ask your four-year-old at 10 p.m. if they would like to go to bed now. Obviously some decisions have to be enforced but the objective should be to get agreement as much as possible and to pass on a love of and passion for a given activity. If you succeed in this, you have passed on a gift for life.

A Reflection on Observation

In my talks to parents I often use little reflections to highlight issues and to make points. One of the reflections I use is called 'When You Thought I Wasn't Looking' by Mary

Rita Schilke Korzan, which is about a child giving feedback to her parents.

When You Thought I Wasn't Looking
When you thought I wasn't looking
You hung my first painting on the refrigerator
And I wanted to paint another.

Most parents can recall the day their child arrived home from crèche or school with their very first paining. This first 'painting' is usually just hundreds of lines scribbled across a page in many different colours, but no parent would say to their child "What is this?" Instead, like the parent in the reflection, we praise our child: "Did you paint this? You're brilliant! I'll hang it up in the kitchen now." In return, our child is delighted. Ten or twelve years later, however, when the child is sent to private art classes at €10 per session, the reaction is very different. In this situation, when the child arrives home with their first painting their parent expects a masterpiece in return for the cost of the classes. The conversation is more likely to follow this path: "What's that? Well you're no artist; €10 for that! Some 'teacher' that teacher is!" It is astonishing how €10 can change the attitude and expectations of parents. How many of us can see ourselves in this dialogue?

One of the main reasons for our change of emphasis is because new issues come into play like value for money. We have different perspectives on and higher expectations of our children as they get older. When our children are small our expectations are simple and very much child-centred as our whole focus is on their interests and happiness, and so we respond positively to their efforts. As our children grow older our whole approach seems to change and factors like our children's enjoyment of activities become less and less significant and are replaced more and more by a focus on standards and performance. A far better approach is to balance factors like your child's happiness, enjoyment and personal interests against performance, achievements, standards and potential. For example, your child might never be a wonderful artist but they could love art and get hours of personal enjoyment and satisfaction out of it, along with developing new friendships with other children involved in art and, in particular, loving the creative and artistic environment of the art world. So a major factor is enjoyment; if your child enjoys an activity then it is very worthwhile and you should support and encourage them to continue their involvement simply for their enjoyment. Being gifted and talented in a particular activity is just the icing on the cake. Children do not need to be geniuses at an activity in order to get benefit and enjoyment from it. I am well aware that life is not based on enjoyment alone but the more things in life that we enjoy the more contented we are with our lives.

When you thought I wasn't looking
You fed a stray cat
And I thought it was good to be kind to animals.

What happens when a stray cat visits your home or garden? If you treat animals with cruelty it is not surprising when your child imitates this behaviour by picking up a stick and beating a cat. We can often be hypocritical by telling our child not to be cruel to animals while we model cruel behaviour ourselves.

When you thought I wasn't looking
You baked a birthday cake just for me
And I knew that little things were special things.

Kindness, in my opinion, is one of the greatest gifts we have to give. If kindness does not get the best out of other people, young and old, then nothing works. I am not talking here about materialistic kindness, I am talking about human kindness – kind words, kind gestures and kind acts. I urge you never to be miserable with kindness and never compromise or sacrifice kindness in any dealings with your children, even when dealing with issues of disobedience or discipline. Kindness should never be withdrawn or reduced. Acts of kindness are never forgotten; kindness speaks every language and is fully understood by people the world over. When do we appreciate kindness the most? On those occasions when we feel down, depressed, alienated, rejected, or hurt physically and emotionally, indeed on all occasions when we are struggling with life. The lower in life we feel the more we long for and appreciate human kindness. Kindness never fails.

When you thought I wasn't looking
You said a prayer
And I believed there was a God that I could always talk to.

This section is self-explanatory – if you believe in God and pray regularly then prayer can be a very good outlet for your children. At the end of the day this is a very personal decision, especially if you have very young children. As your children grow older they will gradually make up their own minds regarding religion and prayer. Religion should never become a conflict issue between parents and their children. You should continue to hold your own personal views and have ongoing dialogue with your children on religious matters but once your children reach the age of fifteen or sixteen years they should be allowed to decide for themselves what they believe and practice. Trying to force your children to attend religious services is bound to cause stress for you and them, and it is very likely that your relationship with your children will be damaged. Additionally, no long-term benefits will accrue for your children as they will most likely opt out at the first opportunity.

When you thought I wasn't looking
You kissed me goodnight
And I felt loved.

As parents we hug and kiss our small children frequently. Children love and appreciate this physical contact as it makes them feel loved. However, problems often arise as our children grow older and become teenagers. At this age most teenagers will feel embarrassed when their parents hug or kiss them in public. As parents you must understand this and accept that it is part of the growing independence of your older children. However, a hug and a kiss is still by far the most powerful way to tell your children that they are loved. This is especially true when your teenager is going through a tough time; a hug and a kiss from you conveys the clear message that you still and always love them. So please do continue to hug and kiss your teenagers on a regular basis, but do it privately where your teenager will feel more comfortable.

When you thought I wasn't looking
I saw tears come from your eyes
And I learned that sometimes things hurt —
But that it's alright to cry.

This reflection highlights a major difference between the genders. I think it is accurate to say that most girls and women of all ages are generally better able to deal with emotional issues. They talk to each other about their emotions and they are not embarrassed to cry openly when they are upset. They also more readily comfort one another. A good example is when a teenage girl is upset and cries in class the normal reaction of her peers is to get her a tissue and a glass of water, to sit down with her, hug her and listen to her, and in a few minutes everything is back to normal with little or no embarrassment. This culture and attitude is great for women. Now contrast this to the culture for men.

Generally in Irish culture men see crying as a sign of weakness and softness. Of course it is nothing of the sort but most men are brought up with this belief. From a very early age this is communicated to boys. When playing sport if they receive a knock and start to cry they are told very firmly, usually by their fathers, to 'toughen up'. Their sporting heroes are often put forward as examples of this toughness: "Brian O'Driscoll doesn't cry when he gets a knock" or "You don't see Henry Shefflin crying, do you?" It is not surprising then that most men grow up feeling that showing their emotions is also a sign of weakness. Of course it is not but this male culture is very difficult to break down. Looking back to the example of the teenage girl crying in class, what would happen if it was a teenage boy who was crying? How would his classmates react? The likelihood is that he would be teased and laughed at and embarrassed. Even more serious is the real possibility that he would be bullied. Other boys would see him as a soft touch and exploit this perceived weakness. Naturally boys are aware of this possibility and so they protect themselves by not showing their emotions; they just suppress them. Attitudes are definitely improving but there is still a long way to go. Parents of boys need to be very sensitive about this whole issue and regularly reassure them that showing emotion is very natural, human and positive thing. This element of Irish male culture needs addressing and it is up to all adults, especially men, to give leadership. Perhaps a good way to start would be for men to show their emotions publicly when it is appropriate.

When you thought I wasn't looking
You cared
And I wanted to be everything that I could be.

When I am talking to parents I always ask the group "Who cared the most when you were growing up?" Overwhelmingly the response is "parents". To highlight this fact I often give the example of the parents of teenagers who live six miles from Dublin city centre. When the teenagers go out on weekends to recreate in places like Temple Bar, in the city centre, their parents can hear them getting into a taxi at 3 a.m. six miles away, they can hear them getting out of the taxi outside their home and they can hear them walking up the pathway to the house. The giveaway is usually the opening of the front door – if they spend time searching for the key or trying to open the door, a parent would arrive down the stairs to check and very often an argument would follow. The parent would want to know why they are so late coming home and perhaps say that they were worried about them. The teenager responds with "Go back to bed", "You have a sad life" or "Who asked you to get up?" The one certainty is that at that particular point they will not be thanking the parent for caring about them.

Teenagers are unlikely to ever fully recognise the genuine concern of their parents but they are lucky to have someone who really cares. However, I believe that they do appreciate it deep down and feel good that their parents are keeping an eye out for them. Also, I believe that because teenagers know that they are being monitored by their parents this encourages them to behave more responsibly than they would if they felt that nobody cared, e.g. they will get home at a more reasonable hour or they will want to arrive home sober. The truly unfortunate teenagers are the ones who can stay out all night and nobody cares or misses them.

When you thought I wasn't looking –
I looked ...
And wanted to say thanks
For all those things you did
When you thought I wasn't looking.

– Mary Rita Schilke Korzan
From the book *When You Thought I Wasn't Looking: A Book of Thanks for Mom.* Copyright © 1 March 2004, Mary Rita Schilke Korzan. Reproduced with the permission of Andrews McMeel Publishing, LLC. All rights reserved.

The central message of this whole reflection is that children observe everything said and done by their parents and so we should always be conscious of this.

The Perfect Parent

Parenting is by far the most complex, demanding, responsible and time-consuming job any person takes on in life. There is no end to the list of skills and competencies that parents are expected to have and need on an everyday basis. I cannot think of any other task in life that is so demanding, and yet the majority of parents receive no training or preparation for it. Despite this fact, however, most young parents are not keen to accept help or advice on how the job should be done. Most of us are just thrown in at the deep end and learn as we go along. We depend hugely on how our parents before us parented. While most of us do our very best, naturally we all make mistakes along the way. There is no such thing as the 'perfect parent', yet many parents feel inadequate and struggle to cope with the many challenges they face every day of the week.

Furthermore, often when parents believe that they have conquered the task with one child they soon discover that the same approach does not work with their second or third child. The reason for this is simple – every child is unique and often very different to their siblings; sometimes only their surname is the same. It is for this reason that I emphasise how important it is to treat each child as an individual, to fully accept their differences and never to compare children; they are all so different, just as we all are. Because of this I have great difficulty with the attitude that all problems with young people stem from their parents. In my opinion and experience this belief is unfair and does not stand up to scrutiny. I often hear people say things like, "Well I blame the parents" or "Why don't his parents make him do it?", as if parents had the capability and capacity to physically force a teenager to do anything. When you are faced with the obstinacy and stubbornness of a teenager you soon realise how impossible it is for a parent to force anyone to do something they are opposed to. While of course parents have a substantial responsibility for the behaviour and general attitude of their children, the line must be drawn at some stage and responsibility handed over to the teenager. I believe that this is vital – young people must be held personally responsible for their actions. Parents can only do so much and the rest is over to the teenager.

A large part of parenting is to prepare your child to take personal responsibility and in particular to be answerable for their decision-making, otherwise your child will never become fully responsible for their actions. However, getting that balance right is a very difficult judgement. At what age should a child be given personal responsibility? As I have stated repeatedly, age is not a very reliable factor in making that decision; it depends much more on the maturity of the child and parents are the best judges of this. Handing over personal responsibility is a gradual process spanning many years and developed step by step. All children develop at their own pace and normally they take on the amount of responsibility they are capable of handling. This is one of the main reasons why I keep saying that parents should never compare one child with another. Unfortunately, parents do it all the time, like they are in competition with each other, even over something as simple as how many teeth a six-month-old has. It is absolute rubbish and should be avoided at all costs.

I have to repeat, every child grows and develops at their own pace and they should not be forced or put under pressure to speed it up. This is a factor throughout every child's early life and into their teens. We all grow and develop at our own rate. Parents will find that some children mature very quickly and by the age of fourteen or fifteen they are very capable of making sound judgements about many elements of their life, while others take much longer and some may be still immature at the age of eighteen, when they are legally classified as adults.

I have often commented that one of the most obvious characteristics amongst the prison population was a high level of immaturity and I remain convinced that this is one of the main reasons why most of them got into trouble in the first place. Many young men in their mid-twenties act like twelve-year-olds. Indeed, I met many twelve-year-olds who are much more mature and responsible than many adults in prison.

Preparing your child to take personal responsibility is one of the main functions of parenting, but it should be nurtured and encouraged rather than enforced or taken for granted. Much of this is basic developmental stuff. Your child should be given responsibility gradually, starting off at a very young age – perhaps giving them responsibility for taking care of their own toys or sports gear. The approach is pretty straightforward – simply tell your child, "This is yours so take good care of it." Some children are never given responsibility or trusted in their own homes, so it is not surprising that when they move out they act so irresponsibly.

I stated above that there are no perfect parents, but if one could apply the philosophy of this reflection they would be well on their way towards achieving this status.

If I Had My Child to Raise All Over Again

If I had my child to raise all over again,
I'd finger-paint more, and point the finger less.
I'd do less correcting, and more connecting.
I'd take my eyes off my watch, and watch with my eyes.
I would care to know less, and know to care more.
I'd take more hikes and fly more kites.
I'd stop playing serious, and seriously play.
I'd run through more fields, and gaze at more stars.
I'd do more hugging, and less tugging.
I would be firm less often, and affirm much more.
I'd build self-esteem first, and the house later.
I'd teach less about the love of power,
And more about the power of love.
It matters not whether my child is big or small,
From this day forth, I'll cherish it all.

— Diana Loomans

From the book *100 Ways to Build Self-Esteem and Teach Values*. Copyright © 1994, 2003 by Diana Loomans. Reprinted with permission of HJ Kramer/New World Library, Novato, CA, www.newworldlibrary.com.